The Road

THE ROAD TO HELL

J. David Pawson, M.A., B.Sc.

Hodder & Stoughton

LONDON SYDNEY AUCKLAND

British Library Cataloguing in Publication Data
Pawson, David
  The road to hell.
  1. Christian doctrine. Hell
  I. Title
  236.25
  ISBN 0-340-53964-X

Published by Hodder and Stoughton, a division of Hodder and Stoughton Ltd, Mill Road, Dunton Green, Sevenoaks, Kent TN13 2YA. Editorial Office: 47 Bedford Square, London WC1B 3DP.

Typeset by Medcalf Type Ltd, Bicester, Oxon.

Printed in Great Britain by Clays Ltd, St Ives plc.

'The road that leads to perdition is wide with plenty of room, and many go that way.' Jesus of Nazareth (Gospel of Matthew)

'Our friends who long to get rid of the eternal punishment should cease to argue against God and instead obey God's commands while there is still time.' Augustine of Hippo (*City of God*)

'Then I saw that there was a way to Hell, even from the gates of Heaven.' Bunyan of Bedford (*Pilgrim's Progress*)

'The road to hell is paved with good intentions.' Baxter of Kidderminster (quoted by Samuel Johnson and Bernard Shaw)

'Sir, if I believed what you, and the Church of God, say you believe, even if England were covered in broken glass from coast to coast, I would walk over it, if need be on my hands and knees, and think it worthwhile living just to save one soul from an eternal hell like that.' Attributed to 'Charlie' Peace (convicted murderer in conversation with the chaplain in Leeds gaol, before being hanged)

CONTENTS

vii

SCRIPTURE STUDIES

FOREWORD

About five years ago I wrote a personal reminder in my notebook. It reads, 'I must preach more about hell.' I had been thinking about how, in the days of my youth, preachers had regularly impressed upon me that there was a 'heaven to gain and a hell to shun'. I was also feeling some alarm at an apparent lack of the fear of God in many Christians. It seemed to me that many who had become Christians in recent years had been taught about the loving care of Father God; but did they understand that he was also their judge?

In the years that have followed, I don't think the balance has been redressed much and, I must confess, I have not paid much attention to the note to myself. Now my friend David Pawson has come along with a sharp reminder.

Many who read this book will be aware that hell has become a subject of some controversy in recent years. In a recently published letter someone writes, '[hell] is a subject on which I must fight. I could not love a God who would torture people eternally.' David is, of course, very aware of that controversy and writes in chapter 6, 'Hell may be disputed, for obvious reasons, even among believers.'

David Pawson has written about controversial subjects before, but this book has not been written as a contribution to the controversy nor as another voice in the dispute. It is written with obvious compassion, a high regard for God's Word and a godly jealousy for the character of God.

I commend this book without reservation to those people who have reached conclusions similar to the ones expressed in it, but also to those who are still forming their views and equally to those who hold other views.

C. Lynn Green,
Youth with a Mission
Director for Europe, the Middle East and Africa

INTRODUCTION

I once preached to a congregation of dogs, mostly of the breed known as Labrador. It was a guest service and each dog had brought a friend – who was blind! It was an annual gathering arranged by the Torch Trust for those who had lost, or never had, their sight.

When I began to prepare my message, I felt constrained to choose the subject of hell. Part of me resisted the thought. Surely these dear people had suffered enough already. They needed comfort rather than challenge, empathy rather than exhortation. But the words of Jesus kept running through my mind: 'If your right eye causes you to sin, gouge it out and throw it away. It is better for you to lose one part of your body than for your whole body to be thrown into hell' (Matt 5:29; part of the Sermon on the Mount).

That became my text. I told my unseeing hearers that most of the temptations of the sighted come through what the New Testament calls 'the lust of the eyes' (1 John 2:16). I asked them to pray for me because I could see.

There was an elderly lady present, who had never been able to see and bitterly resented the fact. When I spoke of the spiritual handicap of sight, she began to feel pity for those who could see. Her heart was softened and opened to the Lord. Her friends told me that she sang praises all the way home in the coach – and died a few days later, rejoicing in her salvation. The first person she ever saw was Jesus.

This was not the first time I had dared to tackle this awesome subject. My records tell me that I began to do so in the Methodist church at Addlestone, Surrey, in July 1955. Though I had been brought up in that denomination and trained at Cambridge for its ministry, I cannot recall any mention, much less any instruction in,

3

or discussion of, this topic. Such knowledge as I had came from my own study of the Bible.

I suppose each one of us carries a mental picture conjured up by the word 'hell' itself, usually associated with some horrifying experience in our past. Two such come to my mind, both from the time during which this book was written.

The first was in Hong Kong. Jackie Pullinger, that courageous and dedicated English lady who makes Christ real to the colony's drug addicts, took me into the 'walled city' (the wall is no longer there – the Japanese demolished it during World War II and used the rubble to build the present airport runway out into the harbour). I can only describe it as a virtual shanty town, with dwellings piled on top of one another many storeys high. Inside it is dark, dirty and depressing. But what gives it its unique character is the extraordinary fact that there are no laws whatsoever over it, for this small area belongs to no one and is under no authority. Pimps and prostitutes, drug dealers and addicts, gamblers and the infamous triads – all may be found here, plying their degrading trades and exploiting human weaknesses. Later, when I had emerged from the bowels of this dreadful place into the welcome sunlight, I felt I had just visited hell. Yet even there the light of the gospel was shining – in the only brightly lit room I saw, at the very heart of the pile on the lowest level, where Jackie and her colleagues prove that Christ can set the captive free. Thankfully, the 'city' is scheduled to be pulled down (before the colony is returned to China).

The second was in Poland, at a place whose very name makes the blood freeze – Auschwitz! Words cannot describe my feelings as I stood in the hermetically sealed 'shower-room' where thousands of Jews, gypsies and other 'undesirables' were suffocated with deadly Zyklon-B gas. Their hair was cut off to stuff cushions, gold teeth were extracted and sent to the bank, tattooed skin carefully removed to make lampshades, fat melted down to manufacture soap, the skinny remains finally cremated and the ashes sold off as fertiliser. I had to remind myself that the men responsible for this unbelievable barbarism went home to love their wives, play with their children and sing Christmas carols! Otherwise I too would have been guilty of their perverted contempt which treated those made in the image of God as somehow sub-human and unfit to live. Once again, as

4

I came out of the windowless chamber and saw the bright sun in a cloudless sky, I felt I had just returned from hell.

As I write, the words of Robert Browning come to me – 'There may be a heaven,' he said, 'but there must be a hell'. It is a demand for a moral universe. If this life is all there is, then injustice reigns. But if there is a life beyond and it includes retribution for the evil-doer, then it becomes possible to believe again that righteousness rules and that God is good.

To that extent, hell is good news. Even if the wicked escape the consequences and penalties of their crimes in this world, they haven't got away with it. They will get their deserts.

Most would agree that some deserve no less than hell. Mass murderers, cruel dictators, drug dealers, child molesters, wife batterers – we probably all have lists of candidates for the lake of fire.

Why do we never include ourselves? Hell is always for the others! A recent gallup poll revealed that two-thirds of the American population believed in heaven and that they were sure to go there; the same proportion also said they knew someone who was sure to go to hell!

Perhaps this is why the teaching of Jesus about hell is so unpopular. He seemed to suggest that the vast majority of the human race were heading there (Matt 7:13) and for such trivial offences – calling someone a fool or looking at a girl lustfully (Matt 5:22,28).

Such statements make us all feel vulnerable. Isn't that taking things a little too far? Surely most of us are not as bad as all that. Yet deep down lurks the uneasy feeling that if Jesus was right, we could be in serious danger – all of us.

Little wonder, then, that this is the most offensive and least acceptable of all Christian doctrines. We try to ignore it, but it won't go away. We attempt to explain it away, but it keeps coming back. Better to face the truth, even if it hurts. There can be no final comfort in delusions.

This has not been an easy book to write. I have started and stopped a number of times. It is an awesome responsibility, knowing that 'we who teach will be judged more strictly' (Jas 3:1). When my briefcase, containing the sole manuscript, disappeared from an airport car park in Bologna, I wondered whether the Lord was telling me not to publish. Providentially, in answer to many prayers, the police returned everything intact a few days later. I was encouraged to believe it was meant to be published.

But why write such a book at all? It is hardly the way to 'win friends and influence people'! The spirit of the age is certainly not conducive to our subject. Existentialism lives for this world rather than the next. Hedonism seeks pleasure and avoids pain. There are enough troubles to cope with in the here and now; why add distant worries about the there and then?

However, forgetting about hell neither abolishes it nor saves anyone from going there. If there is such a place and there is any risk of a single human being going there, it is an act of compassionate love both to warn those likely to go there and to tell them how to escape such a fate. But who are they?

The major thrust of this book will come as a surprise, even a shock, to many Christians, since it is primarily addressed to them. It is far more likely to be read by 'saints' than by 'sinners', anyway. That is as it should be, for two reasons.

First, the spirit of the age has now invaded and infected the church itself. Believers are becoming preoccupied with temporal needs (both inside the church and outside in society) to the neglect of eternal destinies.

Coupled with this major shift of emphasis is an alarming move away from the traditional understanding of hell as endless torment, even among Bible-believing teachers. Annihilation is the current favoured alternative. The question, 'Where will you spend eternity?' will have to be replaced by, 'Will you spend eternity anywhere?' Challenging this growing trend was one of my major motives in writing.

Second, the warnings of Jesus about hell were rarely aimed at sinners; they were occasionally directed at religious hypocrites (like the Pharisees) but usually at his own disciples, particularly the twelve. This contextual fact seems to have been totally overlooked, even by those who still believe in, preach on and write about hell. Drawing attention to it is probably the unique contribution of this book to the present debate.

The implications are, of course, far-reaching – and very disturbing to those whose security rests on the cliché: 'Once saved, always saved' (a phrase found nowhere in scripture) and who think that 'saved' means no more than 'safe'. Hell is a reminder of the need for holiness as well as forgiveness. Who dare say that such a message is irrelevant to the contemporary church?

I am convinced that the recovery of this neglected truth is vital to the health of Christ's body and essential to the task of completing the evangelisation of all the nations (ethnic groups rather than political authorities). This was my basic reason for putting pen to paper.

The book will probably be no easier to read than it was to write. The opening chapters could be very depressing. The gospel has always been bad news (about God's wrath) before it is good news (about his love) – Paul's letter to the Romans is a good example. It would therefore be as wrong to skip reading the gloomy tones of the first four chapters as it would be to stop reading before reaching the glad tidings of the fifth and sixth.

This last was introduced at the suggestion of a number of friends, including the publisher. They felt that a book on hell needs the 'relief' of heaven. Since I did not intend to make this a general treatise on the after-life, I was reluctant to broaden its scope and at first considered adding an appendix. But heaven is a climax, not an appendix, so I have incorporated a chapter in the main text, using heaven as a contrast ('the reverse') to hell. I trust that readers will understand that the ratio of six chapters on hell to one on heaven in no way reflects the proportion of my thought and speech and is not intended to be a model for theirs. It is simply a reflection of the fact that hell is a greater cause of controversy than heaven, for obvious reasons.

The last part of the book consists of a number of scripture studies (including a number of passages which are either hotly debated or pointedly avoided). As well as providing exegetical evidence to support the general text, it is hoped these will also give the preacher some homiletical material which can be used in the pulpit.

May the Lord give you grace to read the whole of my book. You may find it intellectually demanding, emotionally draining and morally disturbing – but persevere. In reading, as in salvation, blessing awaits those who 'endure to the end'. I could not bear the thought of anyone not reading far enough to know that there is no need for them to find themselves damned in hell. Our wonderful Lord, in his great love and mercy, has done everything he could possibly do to save us from this dreadful fate. I pray that the book will leave you filled with gratitude rather than dread, determined to know that perfect love which casts out all fear. Shalom!

NOTE:

When this manuscript was nearing completion, another appeared on the same subject: *Crucial Questions about Hell* by Ajith Fernando, Sri Lankan Director of Youth for Christ, published by Kingsway and with a Foreword by Jim Packer. It covered the same ground and took the same position as my first three chapters. I was tempted to abandon my efforts and leave a clear field for this excellent publication. However, like every other book on this topic, it failed to deal with the crucial fact that most of Jesus' warnings were given to his committed disciples. Correspondence with the author revealed that this was, as usual, an unconscious oversight, as he had failed to take note of the context of these warnings. Having said that, it was clear that he would have interpreted this data in a similar way to myself, for his response to my drawing it to his attention was: 'In my preaching I certainly warn believers about the possibility of forfeiting their eternal salvation by the failure to exercise persevering faith.' I am grateful to him for his encouragement to go ahead with my book ('There is such a need for evangelical statements on this topic that the more there are the better in terms of the total impact on the Christian community') and gladly recommend his study to my readers.

David Pawson,
Sherborne St John, 1992

1   THE RESIDUE

The following report has recently appeared in newspapers and magazines around the world:

The Gates of Hell Opened?

Scientists are afraid they have opened the gates to hell. A geological group who drilled a hole about 14.4 kilometers deep (about nine miles) in the crust of the earth, are saying that they heard human screams. Screams have been heard from the condemned souls from earth's deepest hole. Terrified scientists are afraid they have let loose the evil powers of hell up to the earth's surface.

'The information we are gathering is so surprising, that we are sincerely afraid of what we might find down there,' stated Dr Azzacov, the manager of the project to drill a 14.4 kilometer hole in remote Siberia.

The geologists were dumbfounded. After they had drilled several kilometers through the earth's crust, the drill bit suddenly began to rotate wildly. 'There is only one explanation – that the deep center of the earth is hollow,' the surprised Azzacov explained. The second surprise was the high temperature they discovered in the earth's center. 'The calculations indicate the given temperature was about 1,100 degrees Celsius, or over 2,000 degrees Fahrenheit,' Dr Azzacov points out. 'This is far more than we expected. It seems almost like an inferno of fire is brutally going on in the center of the earth.

'The last discovery was nevertheless the most shocking to our ears, so much so that the scientists are afraid to continue the project. We tried to listen to the earth's movements at certain intervals with supersensitive microphones, which were let down through the hole. What we heard turned those logically thinking scientists into trembling ruins. It was sometimes a weak, but high-pitched sound which we thought to be coming from our own equipment', explained Dr Azzacov. 'But after some adjustments we comprehended that indeed the sound came from the earth's interior. We could hardly believe our own ears. We heard a human voice, screaming in pain. Even though one voice was discernible, we could hear thousands, perhaps millions, in the background, of suffering souls screaming. After this ghastly discovery, about half of the scientists quit because of fear. Hopefully, that which is down there will stay down there,' Dr Azzacov added.

The story has been traced back to a Finnish paper, but there the trail ends. For reasons which will become apparent later in the book (one of them being that hell is not yet inhabited), the account is highly suspicious and probably belongs to the realm of rumour or hoax. However, it prompts two appropriate reflections.

First, such a tale is more likely to provoke fear in people today than any 'hell-fire' preaching from the pulpit. That is because our age is more impressed with scientific discoveries than scriptural declarations. Even Christians can fall into the trap of offering 'scientific' proofs for biblical truth, unwittingly locating authority in human reason rather than divine revelation. Perhaps we need to recall Jesus' realistic assessment of human scepticism – that those who don't accept the words of the prophets will not even be convinced by meeting someone who has returned from beyond the grave (Luke 16:31).

Second, the absence of any explanation of the concept of 'hell' is striking and deeply significant. The reporter assumes, quite correctly, that most of his readers are already well acquainted with the idea of myriads of human souls tormented by unbearable heat.

Such a picture is deeply rooted in Western folklore. It is probably an example of the most effective communication in the history of the church.

MEDIEVAL TRADITION

In the days when the majority of worshippers were illiterate and the Bible remained a closed book studied only by Latin scholars, Christian doctrines were communicated to the eye rather than the ear – both in a dynamic mode (ritual) and a static one (stained glass, sculpture, painting). Few cathedrals of the Middle Ages lacked a vivid visual reminder of the destiny of the unsaved (the stone frieze above the west door in Swiss Fribourg is typical). Such lurid scenes left an indelible impression. When the fear they engendered was linked with an ecclesiastical claim to sacramental monopoly, the sacerdotal stranglehold on society in those days is easily understood.

The medieval concept of hell has survived almost intact, in spite of the Protestant Reformation. But the method of its communication has radically changed. During subsequent centuries, this sombre truth has been conveyed *verbally* rather than *visually*. There was a precedent for this in the fourteenth century: Dante's *The Divine Comedy* traced a journey through hell and purgatory to paradise. This poetic approach would surface again in Milton's *Paradise Lost* and *Paradise Regained*. But it would be through preaching rather than poetry that the tradition would be perpetuated. Many have heard of, though few have actually read, the most famous sermon on the topic, by the American Puritan, Jonathan Edwards, entitled *Sinners in the Hands of an Angry God*, which stimulated revival across the Atlantic and has been widely emulated, from Victorian preachers to latter-day televangelists.

It has to be said that both the visual and verbal portrayals frequently went beyond the restraints of holy writ. Indeed, the horror of hell is probably more effectively conveyed by the meagre information in scripture than by the detailed descriptions of some expositors. It may even be that some of these attempts to improve its impact have been counter-productive, bringing the whole subject into disrepute and even ridicule. However, a reaction against such crudity is not the only reason why hell is taken less than seriously in contemporary thinking.

MODERN TRIVIALISATION

Hell is still a familiar feature in our mental landscape. Yet the familiarity no longer inspires fear, much less terror. Modern man has come to terms with it – through blasphemy, comedy and existential reinterpretation.

It is ironic that the word itself is far more used outside than inside the church. Together with related curses (like 'Damn you'), it is one of the most common swear-words in daily use. At root, such blasphemies are a form of defiance, a show of bravado, daring the deity to strike one down for using holy words in an unholy way (which explains why most obscenities are drawn from the two most 'sacred' relationships: between man and God, man and woman).

'Hell' is now used so frequently that it is considered no more than a mild expletive. Take the classic example of Charlie 'Dryhole' Woods, who after years of fruitless drilling, discovered the biggest oil gusher in California (eighty thousand barrels a day) and described his find to the media in lively though limited vocabulary: 'It's hell. Literally hell. It roars like hell. It mounts, surges and sweeps like hell. It's uncontrollable as hell. It's black and hot as hell.'

Such sloppy usage debases the word, using a greater threat to describe a much lesser one. Its emotive content can be reduced as much by using it too frequently as by using it too rarely.

Hell is also being trivialised in our day through comedy. Laughter is a defence mechanism, especially to shake off fears (how many stage comics are melancholics in private life). We literally 'laugh it off'.

From 'naughty' sea-side postcards to television 'sitcoms' (situation comedies), jokes exploit the widespread knowledge of the Christian belief. Many are variations of the 'heaven for climate, hell for company' theme. Others include a reference to Saint Peter and the 'pearly gates'.

Again, the concept is debased. Apprehension is at least reduced, and even removed altogether. Humour copes with the intolerable. Reverence and ridicule cannot co-exist. Perfect laughter casts out fear.

A more subtle form of reductionism relates to our existential preoccupation with our present situation. The next world has become unreal and irrelevant. This world is the only one that really matters. We therefore make our own 'heaven' or 'hell' here on earth. There is neither pleasure nor pain beyond the grave.

There are two significant implications of this common outlook. One is the transference of retribution from the eternal to the temporal sphere. The facts of life hardly sustain such a theory. The Bible is more honest with its observation that life here can be quite unjust, the innocent suffering and the guilty prospering (see Ps 73:3-14, for example).

The other is the transference of judgement from the divine to the human realm. It is no longer God who decides our destiny – we choose our own. The supreme sovereignty of theism is replaced by the assertive autonomy of humanism.

Hell is no longer an imposed punishment, but a freely chosen preference – even a right to be defended ('If I want to go to hell, who's going to stop me?'). It is no longer a verdict of the divine will, but a victory of the human will. And man is even free to escape from this hell of his own making – by committing suicide.

A hell that has been trivialised in these three, or any other, ways will no longer arouse fear. But human nature abhors a vacuum, and many other fears have moved into the empty house – fear of AIDS, the bomb, cancer, pollution, redundancy, etc. Surprisingly, the process of dying (which can be painful and humiliating) is now more feared than death itself (which it is assumed leads to oblivion, a welcome relief for many, particularly the elderly).

Self-preservation is one of our most profound and primitive instincts; no cost is considered too great to save life from premature death, especially in a context of sudden disaster. Yet our generation is increasingly sympathetic to euthanasia, the hastening of death for the terminally ill or feeble aged. This apparent inconsistency is explicable when death is understood as deprivation of life, which in turn must be seen to be worth living.

The real fear of death itself springs from a belief in the continuity of conscious existence beyond the grave, coupled with the belief that the quality of that life will bear a direct moral and judicial relation to the way we have lived this life. It is anticipation of retribution which gives death its most painful sting. We shrink from the thought of accountability.

For an older generation, death ushered creatures into the presence of their Creator. Lives would be examined and verdicts announced. 'Man is destined to die once, and after that to face judgement' (Heb 9:27). In the Bible, both events are equally inevitable.

That unbelievers in the world should seek to evade this challenge is at least understandable. A pleasure-seeking generation finds such thoughts extremely unpalatable. But that believers in the church, committed to the truth as God has revealed it, should also become evasive is astonishing. Yet that also is a facet of life at the close of the twentieth century.

2   THE RETREAT

Writing in the sixties, a British journalist observed that: 'Forty years ago we stopped believing in hell; twenty years ago we stopped believing in heaven.' He did not make it clear whether he was referring to society in general or the church in particular, though each influences the other. If sermon content was his primary evidence, his assessment was reasonably accurate.

There were, and are, exceptions. Transatlantic fundamentalists and evangelists have 'kept the fires stoked'. In the United Kingdom those holding a Reformed (Calvinist) theology have been the most consistent in speaking and writing about hell.

But it remains true that in the vast majority of churches, both older denominational and newer independent, hell is rarely if ever mentioned. Ironically, while the world talks too much about it, the church talks too little! There is a widespread retreat from this traditional item of faith. This has coincided with a prolonged decline in church membership (a point we shall take up again in the final chapter).

Has this happened by default or has it been deliberate? Has hell simply been overlooked or was it consciously suppressed?

POINTED AVOIDANCE

The church is even more aware of its traditional teaching than the world. Most denominations keep clear records of their historical credal statements. The change has been quite deliberate.

This may be illustrated from Methodism, which claims to have been 'born in song'. From time immemorial, doctrine has been conveyed in the vehicle of music. John Wesley's brother Charles wrote about six thousand lyrics in the eighteenth century, many of them set to popular jig tunes. The following is typical:

> Love moved him to die,
> And on this we rely:
> He hath loved, he hath loved us: we cannot tell why;
> But this we can tell,
> He hath loved us so well
> As to lay down his life to redeem us from hell.

Early Methodists knew what they had been saved from, for and by whom. Consider the following Wesleyan Catechism ('for children of tender years'!):

> What sort of place is hell?
> Hell is a dark and bottomless pit of fire and brimstone.
> How will the wicked be punished there?
> The wicked will be punished in hell by having their bodies tormented by fire and their souls by a sense of the wrath of God.
> How long will these torments last?
> The torments of hell will last for ever and ever.

If such teaching was made mandatory now, there would probably be a mass resignation from the Methodist ministry!

In other 'branches' of the church there is an obvious reluctance to give regular teaching on the subject. Comments have to be provoked by the challenge to engage in controversy. Most such responses are characterised by a 'de-mythologising' of the biblical language, explaining (away?) the descriptive details as 'symbolic' (though very few go on to define the reality behind the 'symbols'). Consider the following contributions from the Church of England.

Archbishop George Carey of Canterbury, in an interview for the *Reader's Digest*, was asked if he still believed in hell and replied: 'Yes! Hell is separation. Not a burning pit or anything like that, but a place of separation from God for those who are wilful in their rejection of God' (which makes one wonder why Jesus chose the language of 'fire', rather than 'separation').

Archbishop John Hapgood of York, in the diocesan magazine, said he believed that hell was 'an internal experience' and that the 'fires' are based on mistranslation of the Bible. He went on: 'We are well rid of those horror pictures of souls in torment and the devils with their toasting forks which blighted the lives of so many of our forebears' (note how he has caricatured Jesus' language of 'fire' by embellishing it with extraneous details before dismissing it).

Even evangelical Anglicans, holding to the inspiration and authority of the Bible, have shown reluctance to express their views. Only after years of spoken and written silence was John Stott, an acknowledged leader in this stream, provoked by prominent liberal Anglican David Edwards in a published debate (*Essentials*, Hodder and Stoughton) to admit he was an 'annihilationalist' (hell is oblivion; see below). This has encouraged many others to adopt this view or admit they already held it. There has, in fact, been a succession of evangelical Anglicans inclined to take this position (Guillebaud, Atkinson, Wenham, France, Green), though others (Lucas) have held to the traditional understanding.

It is striking that those embracing the new viewpoint have been very tentative in preaching it. Why such caution? It could be that those who have doubts about the traditional teaching are not yet sufficiently sure of their new position to challenge centuries of Christian conviction. Or there may be a fear of risking their reputation as 'sound' defenders of the faith (more likely to suffer among evangelicals than liberals).

Or is it simply that they realise that such revised opinions about hell rob it of its fearfulness and effectively neutralise its potential to affect behaviour. In other words, if hell is not conscious and continuous torment but simply nothingness, there is really no point in preaching it any more.

The evidence points to this last conclusion. Traditional instruction has been knowingly rejected. On what grounds? These may be grouped in two categories: those which are personal and subjective, and those which are theological and objective. We will consider them in this order.

PERSONAL AVERSION

Many simply dislike the whole idea of there being such a thing as hell. They find it uncongenial to the point of becoming intolerable. Their rejection is more intuitive than considered.

Sometimes this is due to an imagined, or even instructed, distortion of the biblical data, which has dwelt on sensational, even sensual, fantasies. An overreaction can be the result of a false presentation.

However, such exaggeration does not explain all intolerance. It is worth exploring why many find it so difficult to consider hell objectively.

It has become customary to see human personality as tri-partite: heart, mind and will. We shall use these three dimensions to further our investigation.

Some have an *emotional* reaction to hell. They find the thought of anyone enduring such torment, especially those they have known and loved, too unpleasant to contemplate, quite unbearable, in fact. Those with the greatest ability to empathise have the biggest problem here. It is sometimes expressed in the protest: 'How could I possibly enjoy heaven while anyone I knew is in hell?' Such anguish is far removed from the naïve hedonism that avoids the unpleasant at all costs, and needs to be taken seriously. It is to share the kind of sorrow that Jesus must have felt over Judas. But in the last analysis one has to decide whether one's 'solidarity' is with the holy Creator or his sinful creatures.

Some have an *intellectual* reaction. The modern mind, considering itself sophisticated and refined, rejects hell as barbaric and primitive. Such methods of dealing with recalcitrant members of the human race are regarded as both crude and cruel – and should not even be discussed in a civilised society. They belong to an obsolete phase in the evolutionary development of human community and it is a sign of our maturity that we no longer need such sanctions.

Some have a *moral* reaction. Psychology and sociology have left their mark. We are considered less responsible for our actions. Life is determined for us by our heredity and environment. Misfits should be considered as patients or victims rather than rebels or criminals. Punishment can only be justified if it is reformatory or deterrent; retribution is an outmoded concept. Sinners should not be made to suffer. They need hospital, not hell.

The implication of these reactions is that hell is quite unacceptable to a well-adjusted, mature, integrated society. Man 'come of age' has left behind such infantile imagery. All three reactions are natural and normal.

However, we still face the problem that we owe most of our knowledge about hell to Jesus himself. He was certainly not an average human being, but who would dare call him abnormal? He has been universally acclaimed as sane, balanced and totally integrated. His ethics are acknowledged as the yard-stick for morality. Yet it was he who warned us about hell, and he alone.

Could it be that it is we who are abnormal? That our reactions reveal the prejudiced predisposition of our own fallen nature? That our root objection springs from the instinctive knowledge of our guilt and consequent dread of a final reckoning?

If this is so, even our 'objective' reservations could turn out to be veiled rationalisations. Let us examine them.

PERSISTENT ARGUMENTS

There is nothing new under the sun – particularly in the realm of attacks on the Christian faith. Over the centuries there have been repeated arguments against the church's teaching on hell, even from within the ranks of her own teachers.

The approach is both theological and logical. Usually based on a premise of one of God's attributes, the deduction is drawn that hell is simply inconsistent with what God has revealed about himself. Three such syllogisms have dominated the field.

Hell is considered incompatible with God's *love*

Believing that his love is the one attribute that includes all others, love becomes the only absolute principle of his behaviour (and therefore of ours). Since we would never send anyone to hell, it is inconceivable that a God whose love is infinitely greater than ours would even contemplate doing such a thing. The argument does, of course, depend on our having a full understanding of what real 'love' is, for only then could we project such feelings on to God. Alas, our definition is often more sentimental than scriptural (what would we do about a relative or close friend who turned out to be a psychopathic killer who needed to be permanently isolated from the community?). Perhaps we need to reconsider the nature of true love, before accusing God of being unloving if he sent anyone to hell.

Hell is considered incompatible with God's *justice*

It is of the essence of faith that God is good, that he must be utterly fair in all his dealings with us. 'Will not the judge of all the earth do right?' was Abraham's daring challenge to the Almighty (Gen 18:25). Therefore the punishment should fit the crime, or at least bear some proportion to it. How can a few years of sin justify eternal punishment? And would not this fail to discriminate between 'light' and 'heavy' sins? Would it not be quite unjust for those guilty of mild misdemeanours to suffer the same fate as those guilty of heinous crimes? In this context the question is frequently asked: 'What about those who have never heard (i.e. about atonement and forgiveness in Christ)?' A sensitivity to injustice is universal to mankind, right from childhood ('It's not fair'). Surely God must have the same outlook, only more so. Of course, this line of argument assumes that we understand the seriousness of sin. But can we be objective about this, seeing that sin is our common experience but holiness is unknown to us?

Hell is considered incompatible with God's *power*

If he is omnipotent then he can do anything he sets his mind to – including finding a way to save every human being. If any humans are finally (and permanently) in hell, then God has failed and must live with his frustration. Hell would be a monument to his weakness, in that his creatures have been able to resist him and have therefore proved stronger than their Creator. Some find a solution to this dilemma in their dogma of 'double predestination': God's sovereign will decided beforehand who would go to heaven and who would go to hell; it was his decision, not theirs (and, since all deserve to be consigned to hell, it is an act of mercy to choose some for heaven). But this theory creates more problems than it solves, protecting his power by introducing an arbitrariness which conflicts with other aspects of his revealed character and desires (1 Tim 2:3, for example).

In fact, all these arguments contain the same fatal flaw. They exalt one divine attribute at the expense of others; they emphasise one part to the detriment of the whole. But God is a complete personality, just and merciful, holy and compassionate, kind and severe. His attributes blend together and qualify each other. Above all, having created creatures of choice, he will not force them to love and serve him, which would defeat his purpose of having a larger family. In the last analysis, human beings are free to resist his Spirit and reject his salvation – for ever.

The decisive answer to these 'objective' criticisms is the same as for the 'subjective' reactions – the fact that it is Jesus himself who told us what we know about hell. His unique knowledge of God was an only Son's understanding of his Father. It would be audacious, if not impudent, to suggest that we have a better grasp of God's love, justice and power than he did. Yet he saw no contradiction between God's attributes and actions. He taught his disciples to 'be afraid of the one who can destroy both soul and body in hell' (Matt 10:28; see Scripture Study A).

Before turning to study Jesus' teaching in detail, there is one other aspect of contemporary thinking to look at. The question may already have occurred to the reader – what do those who reject the traditional concept propose to put in its place?

PROPOSED ALTERNATIVES

There are two contenders for the vacancy: 'liberals' are opting for 'universalism', while 'evangelicals' are opting for 'annihilationism'.

Universalism is the belief that everyone will finish up in heaven. Salvation is universal – it is for every member of the human race.

Some scriptures seem to encourage such optimism. 'I, when I am lifted up from the earth, will draw all men to myself' (John 12:32). 'Just as the result of one trespass was condemnation for all men, so also the result of one act of righteousness was justification that brings life for all men' (Rom 5:18). 'For God has bound all men over to disobedience so that he may have mercy on them all' (Rom 11:32). 'God our Saviour, who wants all men to be saved and to come to a knowledge of the truth' (1 Tim 2:3f). 'For the grace of God that brings salvation has appeared to all men' (Tit 2:11). 'He is the atoning sacrifice for our sins, and not only for ours but also for the sins of the whole world' (1 John 2:2).

Universalist opinions have surfaced throughout church history, from Origen in the third century to Barth in the twentieth. They tend to be linked to the Greek view of man as an immortal soul in a mortal body. The thought that such an 'immortal soul' could finally be 'lost' is firmly rejected. However, it is necessary to distinguish between two variations of this outlook, which might be termed 'ancient' and 'modern'.

The older version was that everybody *will be* saved, sooner or later. This implies a 'second chance' (and a third, fourth, fifth and so on, if necessary) after death (what Tennyson called 'the larger hope'). The fact that Jesus preached to the dead is sometimes appealed to for support (1 Pet 3:18-4:6; see Scripture Study H). In other words, there is no closing date for visa applications for heaven.

If there is any torment (temporary), hell is remedial – even an incentive, since escape is always possible. The gates of hell can be unlocked from the inside. Such a 'short, sharp shock' should be enough to persuade all its inhabitants to leave! This programme must be distinguished from the Roman Catholic dogma of purgatory (which is an involuntary, variable punishment for the saved who are not sufficiently saintly to go straight to heaven; sinners still go to hell).

The newer version is that everybody *has been* saved, already. Christ has accomplished a cosmic redemption. The world does not need to be saved, just enlightened about its new status in this era of Anno Domini. Atonement has rendered judgement obsolete. Such thinking is also conducive to notions of the universal fatherhood of God and the universal brotherhood of man, both of which are very congenial to the 'new age' of humanism.

Pope John Paul II has apparently espoused this doctrine: 'Man – every man without any exception whatever – has been redeemed by Christ and . . . with man, with each man without any exception whatever, Christ is in a way united, even when man is unaware of it' (quoted by Stott in *Essentials*, p.325, Hodder and Stoughton). In preaching this 'gospel', the emphasis shifts from the atonement of Christ to his incarnation.

While such views may seem to be supported by some verses in the Bible, specific texts and the general tenor of scripture both point in a very different direction. The New Testament consistently divides the human race into two categories. People are blessed or cursed, they are saved or lost, they go to heaven or hell. This polarisation may be deeply offensive to the modern mind, but is clearly integral to apostolic doctrine. Evangelicals, unable to accept universalism, have opted for an alternative, annihilationism.

Annihilationism is the belief that only 'saints' will survive and live for ever; sinners will be totally eradicated.

Over against the Greek belief in the immortality of the soul is set the Hebrew concept of the resurrection of the body. Man is a mortal soul who needs an immortal body if he is to live for ever (1 Cor 15:53). Immortality is a supernatural gift of God, not a natural property of man. Sinners will not receive this gift. They will become an extinct species. Again, there are two variations on the theme, which need to be noted.

Some say extinction occurs at the *first* death. Those who have not received eternal life before they die cease to exist when they die. Technically, this view is known as 'conditional immortality'. If it is true, millions have already gone into oblivion.

However, this fails to do justice to those scriptures which clearly speak about a future resurrection and judgement for all human beings, both righteous and wicked. Otherwise, it would be very good news for sinners who don't want to be saved! If they can escape the consequences of their sin until they die, they will have got away with it altogether.

More say extinction occurs at the *second* death. The spirit survives the death of the body, only to be consigned to oblivion after it has been 'raised' at the final judgement.

Opinions vary as to how much conscious suffering will be experienced on the way to oblivion, either before the judgement day (in the intermediate state), during it (the shame and disgrace of being found guilty) or after it (for a variable period). Some think the spirit is unconscious between death and resurrection ('soul-sleep'), which would rule out the first of the three possibilities.

For all the guilty, hell would be a place of incineration rather than incarceration. It ends in nothing, whether immediately or ultimately. Again, it is hard to avoid the conclusion that this would be good news for sinners who don't want to be saved. There is 'a hope in hell' – an end to, and therefore an escape from, its torment.

Support is usually found in the vocabulary of scripture, rather than any specific statements. Nouns like 'fire' and 'death', together with verbs like 'perish', 'destroy' and 'consume', when taken in their plainest sense, surely imply extinction. Greek scholars point out that the word for 'eternal' (*aionios*) means 'age-long' rather than 'everlasting'. The ambiguity of these terms will be examined in the next chapter.

There is also a theological argument which, at first sight, seems to carry considerable weight. It is based on three key texts in the New Testament (which we quote in reverse order to indicate more clearly the logical order of the case). 'At the name of Jesus every knee should bow, in heaven and on earth and under the earth, and every tongue confess that Jesus Christ is Lord, to the glory of God the Father' (Phil 2:10f). 'And he made known to us the mystery of his will according to his good pleasure, which he purposed in Christ, to be put into effect when the times will have reached their fulfilment – to bring all things in heaven and on earth together under one head, even Christ' (Eph 1:9f). 'When he has done this, then the Son himself will be made subject to him who put everything under him, so that God may be all in all' (1 Cor 15:28).

From these verses, it is argued that this total ultimate inclusion of all creatures in the kingdom of Christ and his Father excludes the possibility of the eternal survival of any who have resisted their rule. In passing, it is intriguing to note that universalists use exactly the same references and argument to reach a very different conclusion. The challenge must be honestly faced: how can all things be summed up in Christ and God be all in all, if hell and its inhabitants are still in existence?

Two comments seem appropriate. First, a careful reading of the relevant texts reveals an interesting omission in some of them. While creatures 'under the earth' will acknowledge the lordship of Christ, they are not included in the reconciliation of 'all things' achieved by Christ (Col 1:20) or the consummation of 'all things' in Christ (Eph 1:10); both of the latter are limited to 'things in heaven and on earth'. The word 'all' clearly needs to be qualified by its context in each case.

Second, it is obvious that criminals shut out of society by imprisonment are still under the authority of their sovereign (in the United Kingdom the places of detention are called 'Her Majesty's Prisons'). Some would say that such people are even more under the ruler's jurisprudence than free citizens! In the same way, hell would still be under the rule of God – that is, within the sphere of his universal authority (we shall see that, even when the new heaven and earth have been established and the new Jerusalem inhabited, there are still those who are 'outside' the city; Rev 22:15).

Once again, arguments that appear to be logical, when examined more closely are neither totally consistent with scripture nor totally convincing to the seeker. At this point we had better explain how we intend to proceed from here.

While it has been right and necessary to trace the outline of the contemporary debate and draw attention to some weaknesses in the differing viewpoints, we have deliberately chosen not to answer each position in depth or in detail. This would have made these introductory chapters much longer and probably left the reader in considerable bewilderment. In any case, since this book is primarily written for the disciples of Jesus, it is really quite unnecessary to go to such lengths. For such, the teaching of our Lord is decisive. If other theories are seen to be at variance with his words, properly interpreted, then they cannot be right, however impressive their logic may be.

It therefore seems right at this stage to examine the teaching of Jesus himself. If he clearly taught that any human beings would suffer endless torment in hell, then both the alternatives of universalism and annihilationism are, ipso facto, ruled out as error. So what did he say?

3 THE REALITY

Jesus himself is the prime, if not the sole, source of our knowledge about hell. Without his teaching it would be almost impossible to furnish a description, much less formulate a doctrine.

This must surprise those who seem to delight in driving wedges into scripture, putting asunder what God has joined together, virtually creating 'a canon within the canon' (that is, using one part of the Bible as a standard by which to judge the other parts). For example, many (from the heretic Marcion onwards) have tried to draw a contrast between an angry, vengeful God in the Old Testament with a loving, forgiving God in the New. Even within the New, some have accused Paul of introducing legalistic and judicial notions into the 'simple gospel' of love which Jesus proclaimed. All such distinctions founder on the rock of Jesus' teaching about hell.

However, attempts have been made to neutralise, or at least tone down, his warnings, three of which lay charges of:

1. Unreliable reporting. The gospel record is dismissed as inaccurate. References to hell may reflect the thinking of the early church but may not be attributed to Jesus.
2. Cultural conditioning. Jesus was using contemporary ideas to communicate spiritual principles. For example, the 'parable' of the rich man and Lazarus uses the thought-forms of Jesus' hearers and does not necessarily reveal his own beliefs about the after-life.
3. Existential warning. Jesus was using this threat of hell to motivate his hearers, while being fully aware himself that the threat would never be carried out in practice.

All three 'explanations' include some accusation of dishonesty. Such hypocrisy is more likely to be found in those who propound the theories, disguising the fact that they are really motivated by an intense dislike of Jesus' teaching on this topic. Why are there no such objections to his teaching on love or heaven?

Before we study what he said about hell, we should ask ourselves whether we trust him enough to believe that what he says is the truth. He repeatedly used the phrase: 'Verily, verily' or 'Truly, truly' (in Hebrew: 'Amen, amen'), thus constantly emphasising his veracity. He frequently raised the issue of personal trust in his words. 'I have spoken to you of earthly things and you do not believe; how then will you believe if I speak of heavenly things?' (John 3:12). When speaking about the future he assured his disciples he would never leave them with a mistaken impression – 'if it were not so, I would have told you' (John 14:2). He went on to claim that he not only spoke the truth but was also himself 'the truth' (John 14:6). If we cannot trust such a person's warnings about hell, can we trust what he says about anything else? Since hell is not part of this world, either in time or space, we have no other means of finding out anything about it except by revelation from God. Jesus claimed to bring that revelation and to say nothing that God did not first say to him (John 8:28). That is either the truth or a lie. Each reader will need to make up their mind about this, preferably before going any further.

Once this basic issue has been settled, the recorded words of Christ can be studied. Most references to hell are in the four gospels – in the three 'Synoptics' more than John; and in Matthew more than Mark or Luke (the vital significance of this uneven spread will emerge in chapter 4).

But there are some crucial statements in the last book in the Bible – Revelation. This also contains the words of Jesus, this time what he said after his ascension to heaven.

Almost all our information about hell, therefore, comes from the lips of the one whose knowledge of the Father was that of an only Son. To assert that a God of love would never send anyone to hell is to claim a better knowledge of his character than Jesus himself!

Actually, Jesus didn't believe his Father would consign anyone to hell. He claimed that he himself, the Son of Man, would be the judge who delivered the sentence (Matt 25:41; cf. Acts 17:31). And the decisive factor in reaching the verdict would be the defendants' attitude to Jesus himself, as revealed in their dealings with his 'brethren' (see Scripture Study C).

It is time to look at his description of hell in detail. We shall consider the external environment first, then the internal experience – what the place is like, then what it will be like for the people in it.

FEARFUL DESCRIPTION

Jesus was an excellent teacher. He used metaphor and analogy, starting from the known as a 'picture' of the unknown. Such picture-language makes the truth vivid and real, helping listeners to 'see' the truth.

Sophisticated minds prefer the abstract to the concrete and despise simple analogies, dismissing them as 'mere' symbols. They need to hear the following rebuke, taken from a German book on our subject (*Wat is de Hell?* by Schilder, p.40): 'Let nobody say it is *only* symbolical and *therefore* not so terrible. By mere inversion one could say: if the symbol, the mere picture, is already awe-inspiring, how horrible must the original (the actual) be!'

So how did Jesus 'picture' hell? The answer lies in the name he usually gave to it – Gehenna, which means 'the valley of Hinnom'.

This is a real geographic location, a deep gorge to the west and south of Jerusalem. From it the city is visible, but most of it is invisible to the city. Few tourists visit or are even aware of it.

The valley has a sinister history. At one stage in Israel's idolatrous infidelities it became a centre for the worship of Moloch, an Ammonite deity demanding the sacrifice of live infants in gruesome orgies. Jeremiah predicted that 'the days are coming, declares the Lord, when people will no longer call this place Topheth or the Valley of Ben Hinnom, but the Valley of Slaughter' (Jer 19:6).

Partly for this reason and partly because of its convenient location and depth, the valley became the city's garbage dump. The south gate facing the valley is to this day called the 'Dung Gate', which speaks for itself. All the sewage and rubbish of a large city was 'thrown into' (note that term) Gehenna.

The waste was kept down in two ways – incineration by fire of what was combustible and ingestion by worms of what was digestible.

Steep cliffs confined the heat and the smell (its lowest point was too deep for the sun to penetrate).

I visited it in 1961, when it was still being used for waste disposal. It was a dismal, dirty and disgusting sight, which left me deeply depressed. Since then, the whole site has been cleared, cleaned up and landscaped as a park, where lovers stroll and romance flourishes! An exegetical tragedy but an ecological triumph!

In Jesus' day it also had criminal associations. The corpses of crucified felons were 'thrown into' Gehenna (the ultimate disgrace for a Jew was to be left unburied). This would have been the fate of Jesus himself had Joseph of Arimathea not come to the rescue by offering his own tomb. Even more ironic, it was here that one of the twelve apostles committed suicide by hanging himself. The rope snapped and Judas Iscariot crashed to the valley floor, spilling his guts on what later became known as the 'Field of Blood'. Peter accurately summed up the sordid episode by saying Judas 'left to go where he belongs' (Acts 1:25).

Jesus could hardly have chosen a more appropriate analogy. He is saying that human beings, made in God's image and for his service, can so 'perish' that they are ruined for the purpose for which they were made. The useless are discarded. Hell is God's rubbish tip for wasted lives. Such is the tragic destiny of the 'lost'. But what will it be like for those who come to this dreadful end? Did Jesus talk about the feelings of the people as well as the facts of the place? Unlike some 'hell–fire' preachers, Jesus did not dwell on the lurid details or 'dangle his hearers over the pit'. However, his restrained comments communicate the horror even more effectively. 'Life' in hell would be better described as a living death. Perdition has five dimensions, given below.

It is a place of *physical discomfort*. We need to remember that hell is a real place for people with real bodies (this will be made clearer later in this chapter). The high temperature and consequent thirst can therefore be taken seriously, as can the obnoxious smell (brimstone, or sulphur, is the basic ingredient of many bad odours, especially those associated with decay and putrefaction). Perhaps the most frightening 'physical' aspect is the condition of absolute darkness, so that the sighted will be virtually blind.

It is a place of *mental depression*. One of Jesus' most frequent

29

expressions was 'weeping and gnashing of teeth'. This phrase combines two very different emotions – sorrow and anger. However, they combine in frustration. To know what might have been and can now never be would produce exactly the state which Jesus describes, an anguish uniting sadness and resentment – both of which are self-centred feelings. Incidentally, all this clearly involves continuity of memory.

It is a place of *moral depravity*. It is an illusion that some human beings are inherently worse than others – bestial perverts, hardened criminals. Take the masks off and take the restraining hand of God away and we would all be revealed for what we really are. Paul gives us a glimpse of what happens when men give God up and he responds by giving men up – hidden weaknesses are openly displayed (Rom 1:24-32). Hell will complete this process. To be separated from God is to be separated from goodness, of which he is the sole source.

It is a place of *social desolation*. The existentialist Sartre said 'hell is other people'. But living for ever with one's own self-centred self is worse. Hell may be crowded, but it is possible to be desperately lonely in a crowd, especially if there is a total absence of love, sympathy and kindness. The rich man in Luke 16 (see Scripture Study E) seems to be all alone in his agony, with no one around him to whom he can appeal for pity or help. Jesus described hell as being shut out of a party (Luke 13:28f).

It is a place of *spiritual death*. It is called 'the second death'. Death is separation. Hell is separation from God. It is 'outside'. There will be no worship there, for there will be no God to worship. Prayer will be equally futile. When all contact with the divine has been lost, the human also disappears. The image of God is totally defaced. Personal disintegration inevitably follows.

The absence of God is matched in horror by the presence of Satan, the source of all evil. Thousands of his 'angels' (since their rebellion against heaven, they are known as 'demons') will swell the population, polluting the atmosphere with their foul thoughts, words and deeds. The absence of every virtue will be matched by the presence of every vice. No wonder Jesus addressed those condemned to such company as 'you who are cursed' (Matt 25:41).

In both the gospels and Revelation, the word 'torment' (*basanismos* and its cognates) occurs quite frequently. Akin to 'torture', it signifies conscious pain, whether physical or mental.

It is almost impossible to imagine the *depth* of such torment, but questions are often asked about its *length*. How long will the agony last? Will it ever end? Before we answer that, we need to address another – when will it begin?

FUTURE DISPENSATION

There are two common myths about hell. One is that the place already exists and the other is that it is already inhabited. Neither is biblical. Both have fostered the notion that human beings go to hell (or heaven) when they die.

Like heaven, hell is being 'prepared' (compare John 14:2 with Matt 25:41). Neither was part of the original creation. Both are being made ready for use in the future – after the Day of Judgement, which has not yet taken place.

It follows that whatever stage its preparation has reached, hell is still uninhabited (which is why the story told at the beginning of chapter 1 does not ring true). Two questions immediately spring to mind.

First, where are the devil and his demonic angels right now? The Bible locates them on and around the earth (the prince of the power of the air goes to and fro in our planet – Job 1:7; Eph 2:2) and in 'heavenly places' (where we encounter them when we pray – Eph 6:12). A few of them are already locked up in deep dungeons, awaiting the last judgement (2 Pet 2:4; Jude 6). Only at the end of history are any of them thrown into the 'lake of fire' (Rev 20:10).

Second, where are all the people who have already died? 'Man is destined to die once, and after that to face judgement' (Heb 9:27) – but what happens in between the one event (a different date for each of us) and the other (the same date for all of us)?

To understand the biblical revelation about the future it is necessary to understand that human existence has three phases:

1. Embodied spirit – from birth to death;
2. Disembodied spirit – from death to resurrection;
3. Embodied spirit – from resurrection to eternity.

Spatial questions beginning with 'Where . . .?' are only really relevant to the first and third phases, during which the body locates the spirit.

Heaven and hell are both places for spirits with bodies and belong to the third phase. As of now, they constitute a future dispensation, not yet experienced by any. We therefore need to distinguish between the 'intermediate state' and the ultimate state of human life.

Disembodied spirits in hades

Death separates body and spirit. The body returns to its earthly origin (by quick cremation or slow corruption) and the spirit returns to its heavenly origin (Eccles 12:7).

One thing is quite clear – death is not the end of anyone's conscious existence. Disembodied spirits survive the crisis. John Brown's body may lie mouldering in his grave, but his 'soul' goes marching on.

The Old Testament is not very informative about what follows. The dead 'sleep with their fathers'. Their address is *sheol* (the Hebrew word, translated by the Greek: *hades*), which is a neutral word for the abode of the departed, implying neither pleasure nor pain. It has been described as a station waiting-room at midnight with no trains due until the morning! There is little or no expectancy of any consciousness or communication there.

However, there are clear hints of continued existence. Though communication with the dead was forbidden, the prohibition seems to imply the possibility of doing so. Saul used a medium witch to contact the departed Samuel; the resulting apparition seems to have been the genuine article rather than a 'familiar' (mimicking) spirit. Job had hopes of an encounter beyond the grave (Job 19:26). The Psalmist expects to be taken into glory 'afterwards' (Ps 73:24).

The New Testament transforms these tantalising hints into absolute certainties. Jesus claims that his father *is* (not was) the God of Abraham, Isaac and Jacob, that these three are therefore still 'living', and that Abraham rejoiced to witness Jesus' advent. On the Mount of Transfiguration, Jesus conversed with Moses and Elijah (about the 'exodus' he was about to accomplish in Jerusalem – Luke 9:31). God is the God of the living, not the dead (Luke 20:38).

The phrase 'falling asleep' is still used, but it is clearly now a physical description of the moment of death rather than a spiritual description of the state after death. The spirit can be recalled into the vacant body – as with Jairus' daughter, the widow of Nain's son (just around the corner from Shunem, where Elisha had raised a widow's son) and, supremely, Lazarus of Bethany (after the body had begun to putrefy).

In the 'parable' of Lazarus and the rich man, the latter is conscious and communicating in 'hades' (see Scripture Study E). Jesus tells a dying thief they will be together in paradise on the same day on which they both died – little comfort if they would both be unconscious (see Scripture Study F). Then there is that extraordinary piece of information that Jesus' death released the long-dead from their tombs to wander round Jerusalem, where they were seen and recognised (Matt 27:52f; see Scripture Study D).

The main evidence for the survival of personality beyond death is, of course, Jesus himself who, in a few days, went through all three phases of human existence. Though put to death in the body, he was made alive in the spirit, and between his death and resurrection was preaching to those who had been drowned in the flood in the days of Noah (1 Pet 3:18–20; see Scripture Study H). Both he and they must have been fully conscious and able to communicate. With the keys of hades in his hand (Rev 1:18), Jesus could move freely in and out of the abode of the departed. The gates of hades could not be bolted and barred against him – or his church (Matt 16:18).

Paul did not exactly relish this disembodied phase; he called it being 'unclothed' (2 Cor 5:4). However, on balance, he would rather be 'absent from the body, at home with the Lord'. To die would be gain and 'far better' (Phil 1:21–23), language which such an activist would never use of unconscious 'sleep'!

But where is hades? Or is that an irrelevant question for disembodied spirits? Is it a condition rather than a location, a relationship rather than a region? Does space become relative there? And time, too? Will it seem a long or a short wait?

Is it all one place for all the dead? Why is 'hades' never applied to the righteous in the New Testament? Is 'paradise' a specially reserved section? And is the 'prison' where the rebellious angels are kept in custody another section? Where is 'Abraham's bosom'? And the 'great gulf fixed'? Have the wicked already begun to suffer? Are some already comforted and others discomforted? Is hades a foretaste of hell?

Though we would love to have and give answers to these and many other such questions, the fact is that the Bible gives us very little information about this intermediate state, other than to comfort believers that they will be 'with the Lord'. What are we to make of this paucity of information? If we believe that the Bible contains everything we need to know for our salvation, it is clear that it is quite unnecessary to know any more about this intermediate state. It could even be undesirable, focusing our attention, and therefore our hope for the future, on the wrong 'place'. In other words, scripture treats the intermediate as an interlude – and so should we. To become excessively curious about the present whereabouts of the dead might lead us into that desire to have contact with them which God, in his wisdom, has declared distracting and dangerous for us.

The major emphasis in the Bible is on the ultimate rather than the immediate future – which is far more important precisely because it is far more permanent.

Embodied spirits in hell
Resurrection reunites body and spirit. It is of the essence of the Christian faith to say: 'I believe in the resurrection of the body.' But what does this mean?

It is not *reincarnation*. This Eastern notion teaches that we return to this world as someone (or something) else, with a new identity. According to our deserts, the next existence will be better or worse than this.

It is not *immortality*. The Greek concept of an immortal soul released from a mortal body is far removed from the Hebrew concept of a mortal soul putting on an immortal body (no wonder the Athenians ridiculed Paul when he spoke of this, Acts 17:32; cf. 1 Cor 15:53). Immortality is not a natural attribute of man, but a supernatural act of God.

It is not *resuscitation*. It is not a reviving of the old body, which later has to die again (as with Lazarus) but the creation of a new body which never dies again (as with Jesus, so far the only one to have such a 'new' glorious body – with new clothes, too!). The body that is buried (or cremated, or even totally destroyed) is not the body that will be raised at the resurrection (1 Cor 15:37–44).

God could do either of two things with a disembodied (albeit conscious) spirit. He could annihilate it (since it is mortal) or he could immortalise it (by embodying it again, this time in an immortal body). The big surprise is that he has chosen to do the latter, not only for the 'righteous', but for the 'wicked' as well. *All* disembodied spirits are to be re-embodied. This 'general resurrection' is predicted by the prophet Daniel (Dan 12:2), affirmed by Jesus himself (John 5:29), asserted by the apostle Paul (Acts 24:15) and linked to the last judgement in John's Apocalypse (Rev 20:5). It is implied in many other passages (Matt 5:29f; 10:28; 12:41f; Luke 14:14; 20:35; etc.).

At the last judgement both 'death' (which causes spirits to become disembodied) and 'hades' (the abode of disembodied spirits) are themselves thrown into the 'lake of fire' (Rev 20:14). Since both are 'things' rather than persons, the implication is that the flames will consume rather then torment them. In other words, the era of disembodied spirits will be over; from then on all human existence will be embodied, incarnate.

Hell then belongs to the future, not the present. No one is in hell yet, not even the devil (if he were, he could have no influence on earth). We have answered the question: when will hell begin? At the Day of Judgement. When will it end? Will it ever end? That is the crucial issue we must now examine.

FINAL DURATION

The description of hell clearly implies a conscious experience, best described by the word 'torment'. Having explored the depth of this suffering, we now consider its length. How long will the torment last? Three answers to this question have already come to our attention.

Some think it will be extremely *brief.* They suppose it will be no longer than fire normally takes to cause death. Conscious torment will therefore be largely mental and occupy the interval between announcing the verdict and carrying out the sentence.

Others imagine it will be rather more *prolonged.* Biblical hints about differing degrees of guilt and variation in punishment (for example, in Luke 12:47-48) are interpreted in terms of assigned periods of time to be served. However, whether short or long, the punishment will end with release – into heaven (according to the universalist) or into oblivion (for the annihilationist).

Most have understood it to be *endless*. This has been the traditional view of the church for many centuries. But is it the true interpretation of scripture? The Protestant Reformers certainly thought so, as did the Roman Catholics before them. However, an increasing number of contemporary scholars, including evangelicals, are questioning this assumption.

Before examining the data, it may be helpful to simplify the discussion by posing a clear alternative (on the ground that once the basic issue is settled, all the variations will be clarified). The real question is: does the torment of hell come to an end (whether sooner or later) or is it endless? Does hell belong to the finite world of time or the infinite world of eternity? To put it bluntly, even crudely, is being 'thrown into hell' more akin to being incarcerated in a concentration camp or being incinerated in a crematorium?

When biblical language and imagery are first read, the immediate impression is that life is extinguished in hell. Fire is normally destructive, leaving whatever it consumes unrecognisable. Burning has commonly been used to execute criminals. Death is comparatively quick (far more so than crucifixion, which took between two and seven days) and minimally painful (the victim often suffocating through smoke or lack of oxygen). Would not the 'lake of fire' (or 'sea of flames') have the same result?

Other words seem to support this speculation. Jesus said that body and soul would be 'destroyed' in hell. Further, since the first death brings existence in this world to an end, will not the 'second death' bring existence in the next world to an end?

God himself is described as a 'consuming fire', in both the Old and New Testaments (Deut 4:24; Heb 12:29). It would seem a little odd if hell did not 'consume' whatever (or whoever) was thrown into it.

In the light of this, it is at least understandable that some Bible students have embraced annihilationism. The thought could be said to be implicit in the wording, even if it is not explicitly stated.

But it's not quite as simple as that. Words can carry different meanings, depending on the context in which they are used. Theology cannot live on terminology alone! Supernatural revelation requires more than natural reason to unlock its secrets.

For example, while fire usually 'burns to ashes', there are biblical examples of it behaving quite differently. Moses was surprised that the bush was not 'consumed', though the flames were real enough; Shadrach, Meshach and Abednego were not even singed in a white-hot furnace (if the first case was not 'natural' fire, the second certainly was). It may be difficult for man to control fire but God has no problem doing so (as when he directed it at Elijah's altar on Carmel).

It would be perfectly possible for God to limit the 'physical' effect of fire to intense heat and discomfort, which seems to be the exact situation of the poor rich man in Luke 16; see Scripture Study E). It may also be pointed out that those who believe the time of torment will be varied before it ends have already accepted in principle that the fire is not 'natural', at least in its effect.

So the concept of 'fire' in hell is ambiguous. Our earthly experience cannot have the last word in our exegesis. Sooner or later all 'natural' fire burns up all its fuel and dies out. Jesus specifically spoke of hell-fire as inextinguishable (it 'cannot be quenched'). He also mentioned worms which never die (so they are not 'consumed' by the flames either). John speaks of everlasting smoke ascending (Rev 14:11); it is at least puzzling why this should be, long after the fire has finished its task of destruction.

Surprisingly, the word 'destruction' is also equivocal. The most frequent Greek word is *apollumi* and its cognates. Certainly, this can be used for the utter destruction of a person or thing, so that they virtually cease to exist. But this is not its only meaning or usage.

It is the adjective used to describe the 'lost' sheep, the 'lost' coin and the two 'lost' sons (in Luke 15). It is used of the 'spilt' wine (from the split wineskin) and the 'wasted' perfume (which Mary poured over Jesus), as well as the 'leftover' food (after feeding the five thousand). Clearly, the word ranges over a wide spectrum of meaning – from being ruined beyond recovery to being rendered unavailable for use. The English word 'perish' (used in John 3:16 to translate the same word) is not dissimilar in its range. It can mean 'cease to exist' (as in 'thousands perished in the earthquake') or 'become useless' (as in 'this hot water bottle has perished').

Even the word 'death' may be taken in different ways. It can mean spiritual deadness, as in the case of Adam (Gen 2:17) and his descendants (Eph 2:1). The prodigal son was 'dead' (to his father) while he was in the far country (Luke 15:32). Even when used in a physical sense, it does not necessarily include extinction. If the 'first death' does not terminate the conscious existence of the individual, the 'second death' need not inevitably do so.

So far the evidence is inconclusive and could be interpreted either way – to continue or to cease to exist. We turn now to a word which at first sight might seem to settle the issue (and, indeed, does for many) – the word 'everlasting'. This is applied both to the fire itself and the punishment it inflicts (Matt 25:41 & 46). That exactly the same adjective is applied to 'life' in the same passage has been one of the most frequent arguments for the traditional view that torment in hell is endless.

Recent writings have challenged this conclusion in a number of ways. One approach prefers the translation 'eternal', claiming this refers to a quality rather than a quantity of life (or death). Majority opinion now favours a combination of both quality and quantity.

The Greek adjective (*aionion*) is derived from a noun (*aion*, from which we get our 'aeon'), which certainly refers to a period of time – an 'age' or an 'era'. The adjective therefore means that which is characteristic of that whole age, or that which is 'age-long'. This can then mean either a limited or unlimited period of time, depending on whether the 'age' referred to is finite or infinite. In New Testament thinking the 'present evil age' is limited in time, but the future 'age to come' is unlimited. From which of these two ages does hell derive its character, from the age that is passing away or the age that will endure for ever?

The adjective is used over seventy times in the New Testament. Nearly sixty of these, applied to both persons and things, clearly indicate a permanent state (forty-three qualify the 'life' made possible through Jesus Christ, which is assumed to continue for ever). Likewise, when it is used to qualify attributes of God it is assumed that they are his permanent characteristics. Only seven times is it applied to the punishment of sinners. But does it then mean age-long or everlasting, lengthy but limited or endless?

If the word itself leaves the question open, there is one New Testament phrase which does not allow any debate, that is, 'to the ages of the ages' (in Greek: *eis tous aionas ton aionon*), which translates into English as 'for ever and ever'. There could be no more emphatic expression in the Greek language for what we understand by endless time. Since scripture applies this phrase to hell, it might be expected to silence the annihilationists.

Not so! While admitting, often reluctantly, that the punishment must therefore be 'everlasting', they then draw a distinction between the *effect* and the *experience* of the punishment, the former only being the endless part. Sinners are annihilated, not tormented, 'for ever and ever'.

Apart from appearing to be a rather superfluous use of words (could annihilation be any other than permanent?), there is one reason why such a distinction cannot be drawn from the biblical data. The phrase 'for ever and ever' is used in the New Testament to qualify 'torment' as well as 'punishment' (Rev 14:11; 20:10); and we have already noted that the former word refers to the experience rather than the effect of the punishment and can only mean conscious suffering (we shall return to this point later).

Before moving on to look at some of the clearest evidence in scripture, we may pose four questions which annihilationists must face.

First, why should the wicked be 'raised' (i.e. given new bodies) for the Day of Judgement, only to have them destroyed again immediately afterwards? This would be a totally unnecessary act of creation and seems somewhat bizarre, to say the least. Unless disembodied spirits are totally unconscious (some cults believe in such 'soul-sleep', though Christian orthodoxy has usually rejected this view), there would be no need for them to be resurrected. The Lord could judge and sentence their spirits to annihilation (in much the same way as Jesus preached to them, 1 Pet 3:19–4:6; see Scripture Study H). Giving them bodies again would create the further need of creating a place to dispose of them! This leads on to the second question.

Second, why 'prepare' a place called 'hell' at all? The God who created the whole universe by his word can surely obliterate it with the same instrument. 'Fiat' creation can be followed by 'fiat' destruction. If the Son could kill a fig-tree by cursing it, the Father could surely do the same to any part of his universe. Why go to the trouble of constructing an incinerator?

Third, what is to be made of the clear statements that the fire, smoke and even worms of hell are permanent? This implies their continued existence long after their function has been fulfilled. What possible purpose could they fulfil after their victims have been exterminated? The surprising answer from some annihilationists, acknowledging that hell is permanent, even if its inhabitants are not, is that hell will serve as a 'memorial'! But to whom will it be a reminder and why will they need to be reminded? The Lord hardly needs that. Would the saints experience more joy or gratitude if they could see hell from heaven? Is there any scriptural basis for such extraordinary speculation?

Fourth, why should the thought of oblivion inspire fear? Jesus spoke with utter horror of Gehenna. Any sacrifice (of organ or limb) was preferable to finding one's 'whole body' in that dreadful place. It is a fate worse than death. It would be better never to have been born. Fear of hell far outweighs the fear of death (Matt 10:28; see Scripture Study A). Thoughts of annihilation do not inspire terror and can even be a welcome idea. Perhaps this is why those who believe it rarely preach it. Oblivion may be something to postpone as long as possible, but most would probably accept it quite stoically when it finally comes. And sinners who have had their fling would probably be glad of it.

Apart from these niggling problems, there is one major weakness in the annihilationist scheme – and indeed, in most debates about hell: the focus of the discussion is usually the ultimate destiny of human beings. This concern with our own future is understandable (we have so much to lose) but it distorts the debate. For hell was never intended or prepared for the human race. It was 'prepared for the devil and his angels' (Matt 25:41). Why for them?

God faced a problem when the angels, led by Satan, rebelled against his rule (Rev 12:4 seems to indicate a third of them). For they were a superior species to Homo sapiens, especially in one important respect. Whereas human beings were mortals capable of receiving immortality, angels were created inherently immortal. Unlike God, they did have a beginning, but like God, they would have no end. As Jesus said, they cannot die (Luke 20:36; note that after the resurrection, human beings will share this immortality, though they do not have it before, even though their spirits survive death). This is why angels are not born, do not marry and reproduce, as we do. Their number (which is huge) is fixed.

Since these rebellious angels could never be annihilated, God had to prepare a place for them to be isolated from the rest of his universe. As we have already made clear, they are not yet consigned there, though the worst offenders (those who seduced human women; Gen 6:1f) have already been taken into custody to await trial (2 Pet 2:4; Jude 6; see Scripture Study I). The dungeon is significantly called 'tartarus', a word borrowed from Greek mythology, which distinguishes this place of confinement from both hades and hell.

Following the final judgement, these rebellious angels (demons), for whom there is no hope of forgiveness or salvation (Heb 2:16), perhaps because they had already known life in heaven and rejected it, will join their leader in the 'lake of fire' and share his 'everlasting punishment'.

What is that punishment? To cease to be for ever or to continue to be for ever? Scripture is crystal clear on this point. It says of the devil that he will be '*tormented* day and night for ever and ever' (Rev 20:10; literally, 'to the ages of the ages'). It is not good enough to dismiss this verse as 'difficult' (just because it doesn't fit a particular theory) or as 'symbolic' (without explaining what it symbolises), as annihilationists are prone to do (I am quoting actual comments, without naming the authors). If language means anything, the devil and his angels do experience endless suffering in hell.

Some are prepared to admit that this is the fate of fallen angels, while still denying that fallen humans will share it. Does scripture allow such a difference to be made? Or does it point to the same fate for all fallen creatures, whether in heaven or on earth?

When the devil is 'thrown into' (the same verb that is used of human beings; Luke 12:5) the 'lake of fire', he is joining two beings already there: the 'beast' and the 'false prophet' (Rev 19:20). They are earthly rather than heavenly and have been profoundly affecting human affairs. But are they human beings?

It has become fashionable to interpret them as personifications (like 'Mother Nature') rather than persons. They are supposed to

41

'symbolise' social structures and institutions which affect political and religious life. However, such structures and institutions are devised by humans, maintained by humans and led by humans, with one human often dominating them. The book of Revelation presents the two as 'he' and not 'it'. The rest of the Bible mentions other 'antichrists' (1 John 2:18; note that this verse also mentions 'the' antichrist) and false prophets (Matt 24:11) – but all of them are individual human beings. It follows that *the* antichrist (whom Paul calls 'the *man* of lawlessness'; 2 Thess 2:3) and *the* false prophet are superlative individual examples of both genres. What clinches it is the fact that both are 'tormented'. Since when could social structures be tormented?

So at least two human beings suffer endless torment in hell. But the same book of Revelation assigns a much larger number to the same fate. Of all those who have accepted the branded number of the 'beast' (in order to be able to buy and sell the necessities of life) it is said: 'The smoke of their torment rises for ever and ever' (Rev 14:11; again, 'to the ages of the ages'). Some have tried to say that the smoke will continue to ascend long after their torment is over. But it is not the smoke of the fire that once tormented them; it is the smoke of 'their' torment (we may compare with this Jesus' similar use of the personal pronoun: 'their worm does not die'; Mark 9:44, quoting Isa 66:24). Presumably those referred to here were motivated to identify with the rule of the 'beast' through fear for their lives, which may explain why the 'cowardly' are included in the list of those destined for the 'lake of fire' (Rev 21:8).

The decisive passage is the so-called 'parable' of the sheep and the goats (Matt 25:31–46; it is more prophecy than parable – see Scripture Study C). Every scholar agrees that the animals represent human beings. While the 'sheep' inherit the kingdom 'prepared' for themselves, the 'goats' are sent into the 'eternal fire prepared for the devil and his angels'. This can only mean that those rejected by the Shepherd-king share exactly the same 'everlasting punishment', which we have already established is endless suffering. There is no hint whatever that the fire which torments one group will annihilate the other.

Consistent with this continued existence is the description of sinners as 'outside' the new Jerusalem, rather than totally obliterated

(Rev 22:15). Such 'dogs' will not foul the golden streets. 'Their place will be in the fiery lake . . .' (Rev 21:8). In the gospels, Jesus often used this concept of being 'cast out, thrown out, left outside'. He spoke of it in tones of utmost horror. He considered it the worst thing that could ever happen to a human being.

To summarise, the traditional understanding of hell as endless torment is sustained by scripture, first for the fallen angels and then, by association, for sinful humans. Though some words and even statements are admittedly ambiguous, others are clear and unequivocal. The former should be interpreted in the light of the latter. The fact that much of the clear evidence comes from the book of Revelation is no reason for dismissing it. Perhaps such treatment of it was already anticipated by the solemn warning at the end: 'If anyone takes words away from this book of prophecy, God will take away from him his share in the tree of life and in the holy city, which are described in this book' (Rev 22:19). To reject its statements about hell is to run the risk of discovering the hard way its veracity on the subject! The risk of losing heaven is, ipso facto, the risk of living in hell. But there are many more ways of running this risk, as we shall now see.

4   THE RISK

People who go to hell deserve to be sent there. The Bible everywhere assumes that human beings are responsible for themselves and accountable to God. Were this not so, a day of judgement would be the supreme farce.

We are the result of our choices. Bad character is formed by bad decisions. Of course, heredity and environment have some influence; but that they are not decisive is proved by the numbers who have risen higher or fallen lower than their ancestry or upbringing.

God alone can know the extent of this personal responsibility, for he alone can know all the circumstances. He will be absolutely just in judgement, against which there can be no appeal.

Yet he has delegated this task to a human being (Acts 17:31)! Jesus will decide the eternal destiny of every human being – including those who dared to judge him (Caiaphas and Pilate). Before him will stand all the world's rulers, all founders of world religions, all the world's business magnates, all the world's scientists and artists, statesmen and politicians, philosophers and visionaries, architects and musicians, sportsmen and entertainers, pilots and cabdrivers, engineers and farmers, housewives and models, doctors and nurses – and millions whose names are known only to God. 'For we must all appear before the judgement seat of Christ, that each one may receive what is due him' (2 Cor 5:10). He is the Son of Man, the Shepherd-king who will separate the sheep from the goats, according to their attitude towards himself (Matt 25:31-46; see Scripture Study C).

Some find comfort in the thought that Jesus will be our judge. He was, and still is, human himself and therefore understands both our circumstances and our weaknesses. We can therefore expect a sympathetic hearing. On the other hand, no-one has ever taught such high moral standards. And he demonstrated a unique ability to see right into human hearts (which is why hypocrisy angered him more than anything else).

Each of us will stand before him to give an account of ourselves (and no one else). No witnesses or evidence will be needed, since everything about us is already known and recorded. The trial will not be prolonged – only long enough for the verdict to be given and the sentence pronounced. On what will that depend? The answer is: 'the things done while in the body, whether good or bad' (2 Cor 5:10). So what are those 'things done' in this life which could land us in hell? It is important, even vital, for us to know.

Few people would deliberately choose to go to hell (that would seem an extreme form of masochism). But many choose to travel the road that leads there, either because they do not realise it or do not believe it. Most would not regard their 'sins' as sufficiently serious to warrant such a fate ('After all, no one's perfect') and might even claim that their pleasant indulgences are 'harmless' and therefore innocent. They will be shocked to discover how offensive their attitudes and activities have been in the sight of a holy God. For example, *all* adultery is an indictable offence in divine law, whether physical (sexual intercourse outside marriage), mental (looking with lustful thoughts) or legal (most remarriages after divorce).

If unbelievers are shocked by such comprehensive standards, believers are shocked to discover that the same standards (and penalties) still apply to them, even after they have been accepted by God. Carefree sinners and careless saints are both in for some big surprises. We shall look at the two groups separately, however.

CAREFREE SINNERS

There are many lists of sins in the New Testament. Allowing for overlap, the total number is about one hundred and twenty. Compiling the full inventory is a sobering exercise, remembering that any one of them would be enough to condemn us.

As most would expect, illicit sexual activity figures frequently, both the heterosexual and the homosexual varieties. God, who invented sex, has made it quite clear that its enjoyment is to be limited to one man and one woman bound together in lifelong loyalty.

Alongside unnatural vices appear other sins which most societies would classify as 'crime'. Murder and theft are two obvious examples. The former would include abortion and active euthanasia (but not capital punishment); the latter would include fraud and tax evasion (though not tax avoidance).

Not surprisingly, perverted religion is extremely offensive to God, both in occult form (with its black and 'white' magic, charms and ceremonies, sorceries and superstitions) and idolatry (whether false images or imaginations).

Sins of injustice lie alongside immorality. Exploitation of the needy, suppression of the weak, contempt for the poor, maltreatment of the alien – all are offensive to the God of righteousness. Paul groups slave-traders with perverts and perjurers (1 Tim 1:10; a rebuke to those who accuse him of approving slavery).

Self-indulgence covers a number of offences. Greed is classed as idolatry, for it invariably focuses life on created things rather than the Creator. Covetousness is the only inner (and therefore, hidden) sin mentioned in the ten commandments (and the one which many Pharisees, including Paul, failed to keep; Rom 7:7-8). Drunkenness occurs more than once.

Sin can take the form of words, as well as deeds. False witness (purveying lies or withholding truth), gossip, slander – these are as hurtful to God as to others. One of the things God cannot do is tell a lie; 'all liars' are destined for the 'lake of fire' (Rev 21:8), where they will join the 'father of lies' (John 8:44). Even our 'idle words' (those casual remarks that slip out when we are off-guard) could bring anyone to judgement (Matt 12:36f). Truly, the tongue is a little member 'set on fire by hell' (Jas 3:6) and could take the whole body there.

Then there are the more subtle, and therefore the more dangerous, sins. Uncontrollable temper, habitual laziness and bitter envy are all 'deadly' sins, but pride is the very worst. Nothing separates anyone from their Maker more easily than this. In fact, to be proud is to deify and adore one's self, which is the most obnoxious form of idolatry. It can even be found in those who have achieved a degree of righteousness, or at least outward respectability. Jesus gave clearer warnings about hell to the Pharisees and scribes (Matt 23:33) than to the 'sinners' of his day.

Surprisingly, 'cowardice' is listed (for example, in Rev 21:8). This surely refers to moral timidity, knowing what is right, but fearing the consequences of doing (or even saying) it. Fear of man and fear of God are incompatible.

The list seems endless! As if all this were not enough, there are sins of omission as well as sins of commission – that is, things not done that should have been as well as things done that should not have been.

Two in particular are singled out by Paul, when he says that Jesus 'will punish those who do not know God and do not obey the gospel' (2 Thess 1:8). Clearly, it would be unjust to penalise those who have not had the opportunity to do either. It seems that Paul is here dealing with two groups of people.

On the one hand are those who have heard the gospel, but not done anything about it (it would be inconceivable that anyone would be punished for not hearing the gospel – and scripture never makes such a statement). The word 'obey' is interesting; the gospel is not just to be accepted or believed but obeyed – presumably by repenting and being baptised (Acts 2:38). Unbelief is a wilful act of disobedience (John 16:9; Rev 21:8).

But what about those who have never heard the gospel? This is one of the most common questions which unbelievers ask (ironically, the questioner usually has heard and has neither the desire nor the intention to go and tell those who haven't; their motive in asking seems to be a desire to prove that God is unjust). The Bible gives a clear answer: everyone will be judged by the light they have received. No one will be condemned for not having heard. But that does not mean they are in a state of innocence. Were that the case, missionary evangelism would be more likely to populate hell than heaven! Better to leave them in ignorance than rob them of innocence. But this is not the situation.

They come into the category of those 'who do not know God'. This presumes they have had the opportunity of some kind of relationship with him, even if they have never been told about his Son. They have had two channels of 'general revelation'. The creation outside them and the conscience inside them have communicated some information about the power and purity of their Creator. These invisible qualities have been clearly demon-strated, easily understood and wilfully ignored, leaving men 'without excuse' (Rom 1:20; the first two chapters of this epistle deal with this whole issue). Mental obtuseness is deliberately self-inflicted. It is not that people don't know about God; they don't *want* to know.

We shall, then, be judged only according to the light we have received and how we have responded to that light, however dim it may have been. Those who have responded positively will be accepted and acquitted. But who has? Can anyone honestly claim to have consistently followed even their own conscience, never mind that of anyone else? The whole world stands guilty at the bar of justice. That is why the gospel must be taken to all nations and preached to every creature (see chapter 7).

What about those who have heard the gospel and have responded to it? Can they now forget about hell, at least as far as they themselves are concerned? Many, perhaps most, evangelicals would answer in the affirmative – believers are in no risk or danger; they may lose blessing on earth or reward in heaven, but will never go to hell. Readers who have taken this view are asked to approach the next section with an open mind and an open Bible, asking the Spirit of truth to reveal the truth of scripture.

CARELESS SAINTS

Most of Jesus' teaching on hell is to be found in the gospel of Matthew. How significant is this?

The book has a strongly Jewish flavour, with its special emphasis on the fulfilment of Hebrew prophecies (making it very suitable to be placed nearest to the Old Testament in the New 'canon', though it was probably not the first to be written) and its avoidance of the divine name (using 'kingdom of heaven' rather than 'kingdom of God'). Does this mean that hell is a topic for Jews rather than Gentiles? Actually, this Jewish angle has been over-emphasised. 'Matthew' contains both anti-Jewish and pro-Gentile material – and concludes with the 'Great Commission' to disciple all nations (i.e. all ethnic groups, all Gentiles).

This last is the clue to the real nature of the first gospel. It is a

'Discipleship Manual' to help 'make disciples by . . . teaching them to obey everything I [Jesus] have commanded' (Matt 28:20). The teaching is gathered into five blocs (reminiscent of the Pentateuch, the five books of Moses?) under the theme of the 'kingdom' – its lifestyle, mission, growth, community and future.

'Matthew' was therefore written for use by and in the *church* (it is the only gospel to use the word). It is addressed to disciples, 'sons of the kingdom', who have received Jesus, believed in his name and been born of God (John 1:12; if this verse applies to anyone, it must include the Twelve). And it is to these 'disciples' that Jesus addresses most of his teaching on hell, as if they are the ones who most need to be reminded of it.

This is confirmed by noting the immediate context of the warnings. While it seems clear that Jesus took it for granted that all sinners are heading for hell (e.g. in Matt 7:13; this is even clearer in the gospel of Luke, which was written for sinners rather than disciples – see Luke 12:1,4–5,54), he never explicitly and directly preached this to sinners themselves (chapter 7 will explore the significance of this for our preaching). Twice, he gave a severe warning to the scribes and Pharisees (e.g. in Matt 23:15); how he hated religious and self-righteous hypocrisy! The rest of his dire words, however, were addressed to his own disciples and the twelve apostles in particular. The clearest warning of all was given to those he sent out two by two as missionaries to demonstrate and declare the kingdom; they were to retain the fear of hell themselves, rather than retail it to others (Matt 10:28; see Scripture Study I for an extended exegesis of this crucial text).

The Sermon on the Mount contains frequent mention of hell and destruction; who was it intended for? Most evangelical commentators assert that its exalted ethics are intended for the church rather than the world, for Christians rather than unbelievers – yet they studiously avoid facing the implications of telling 'Christians' that they are in danger of hell-fire and that 'it is better for you to lose one part of your body than for your whole body to be thrown into hell' (Matt 5:22,29). Whether this evasion is unconscious or deliberate, it is both noticeable and significant (see, for example, *Studies in the Sermon on the Mount* by D. Martyn Lloyd-Jones and *Christian Counter-culture* by John R.W. Stott).

The problem is not solved by pointing out that the sermon was probably overheard by the general public (Matt 7:28); it was clearly addressed to the disciples (Matt 5:1). In any case, the incredibly high moral standards demanded here clearly apply to life in the kingdom, difficult even for those who have received divine grace, but impossible for those who have not. It is addressed to 'you' who are the salt of the earth and the light of the world, but who are yet persecuted 'because of me [Jesus]'. In spite of this, the threat of hell is implicit to the whole discourse and explicit at a number of points. The listening disciples must choose between the broad way that leads to destruction and the narrow way that leads to life. They could find themselves on the wrong road through the 'lust of the eyes' (Matt 5:28; 6:23; cf. Job 31:1 and 1 John 2:16), or contemptuous speech (Matt 5:22).

The apostolic authors of the epistles frequently make the same point. Paul more than once warns believers that if they *continue* to practise the works of the flesh, they 'will not inherit the kingdom' (1 Cor 6:9f; Gal 5:19-21; cf. Matt 25:22). The letter to the Hebrews is even more blunt – there is no more sacrifice for those who wilfully go on sinning after receiving knowledge of the truth (Heb 10:26; clearly addressed to believers since the writer includes himself in the risk, as he does in 2:1-3, to say nothing of his notorious warning in 6:4-8). Peter likewise says it is better never to have known 'the way of righteousness' than to turn away from it (2 Peter 2:21f).

The ground of such warnings to believers is divine justice. Would it not be grossly unfair of God to condemn an unbeliever for adultery, while excusing it in a believer? That would show partiality, even favouritism, which may be found in human judges but of which there is no trace in the divine character, as many scriptures testify (see Rom 2:1-11 for a devastating warning to the Roman 'saints' not to be presumptuous in thinking that God would overlook in them what he condemns in others). God must punish sin wherever it is found, inside or outside his people (Col 3:25). Indeed, judgement must begin with the family of God (1 Pet 4:17).

But are not all sins forgiven when we are justified by grace through faith in Christ? Past sins certainly are, but not future ones. There will be later sins; to deny this is self-deception (1 John 1:8). These can and must be dealt with by appealing to our advocate (1 John 2:1) and applying his atonement; as we go on confessing our sins, he will go on forgiving them and the blood of Jesus will go on cleansing (1 John 1:9; all verbs are in the 'present continuous' tense in Greek).

There is a further serious point. Just as the book of Leviticus draws a distinction between unwitting and wilful transgressions of the law (requiring different sacrificial offerings), so the New Testament also distinguishes between accidentally falling into sin (Gal 6:1) and deliberate walking in sin (Heb 10:26). Disciples are not allowed the luxury of complacency.

Returning to Jesus' teaching in the gospels, we find a significant shift of emphasis in the application of hell to believers. As compared to the list of things that could take unbelievers to hell, the bulk of the warnings are now related to sins of omission, things neglected rather than perpetrated, with quite a different range of indictable offences.

The final bloc of teaching in Matthew (addressed only to the Twelve) is about the future of the kingdom, the signs of the return of Jesus and how his servants can be ready for that event (Matt 24-25). In a series of parables Jesus makes the point that their Lord and Master is not so much concerned with what they are doing at the moment of his return, but what they have been doing during his absence, especially if he is away 'a long time' (Matt 24:48; 25:5,19). The real test of our readiness is not what we do if we think he is coming soon but what we do if his coming is delayed.

In his disciples, the absent Lord expects *vigilance* (like bridesmaids with enough oil in their lamps to keep burning until the bridegroom comes), *diligence* (like good businessmen trading their talents) and *benevolence* (feeding, clothing and visiting his 'brethren'; see Scripture Study C for who these are).

The alarming aspect of these parables told to the Twelve is the verdict on and sentence given to those who have not been faithful in their duties. The servant who neglects his duty and abuses his colleagues is 'cut to pieces and assigned a place with the hypocrites, where there will be weeping and gnashing of teeth' (Matt 24:51; note that 'cut to pieces' does not end his existence!). The servant who buried his talent (because he was only given one?) is accused of being wicked, lazy and worthless – before being thrown into the darkness, where there will be weeping and gnashing of teeth (Matt 25:30). Those who have shown no concern for their master's brethren are cursed and banished to everlasting punishment in everlasting fire, prepared for the devil and his angels (Matt 25:41,46). All this is the language of hell, though the word itself is not used.

And all this is said to the twelve disciples (Matt 24:1), not to the public in general or sinners in particular. Though in one case bad things were done, in every case good things were not done. Discipleship is not to be taken lightly; it carries responsibilities as well as privileges.

It is a sobering thought that one of those twelve, who had preached and healed in the name of Jesus, came to such a dreadful end and went to where he belonged (Acts 1:25). Judas Iscariot was called by Jesus, responded to that call, walked with him and ministered for him over three years. Yet Satan 'entered into him', finding the ground for doing so in his greed for money. He who could have been a son of adoption finished up as the son of perdition (John 17:12).

No wonder the apostolic writers constantly exhort believers to be sober and watchful, confident in the Lord but not in themselves. There is a false confidence that borders on complacency: 'So, if you think you are standing firm, be careful that you don't fall' (1 Cor 10:12; drawing out the lesson for believers from the failure of so many Israelites to make it to the promised land).

It is time to summarise this chapter. Both believers and unbelievers have reason to be reminded of the dangers of hell. But if the teaching of Jesus is our guide, it is *more* needed by those committed to following and serving him. This conclusion, based on contextual considerations, is in sharp contrast to the traditional application of the doctrine. Not only does this bring a fresh perspective to our understanding; it may remove one of the main reasons why preachers find the subject so distasteful and their hearers find it so offensive (see chapter 7).

For both believers and unbelievers it seems so easy to go to hell and so hard to get to heaven (actually, Jesus himself would agree; Matt 7:13-14). Considering the many things done or left undone which could take us there, hell would seem not so much a risk as a dead certainty – if we are left to ourselves. But we have not been left to ourselves. The entire resources of heaven have been made available to us. There is no need for anyone to finish up in hell. So far, this book has been mostly bad news. Now for the good news!

5 THE RESCUE

No book on hell would be acceptable to God or any man without a chapter on how to avoid going there. If there were no way of escape, it would be better to keep silent about the whole subject. Those who are destined for hell could then at least be allowed to enjoy the pleasures of sin for a season, without the nagging thought that they will all have to be paid for one day. Why spoil their temporary happiness with disturbing ideas of eternal misery? Ignorance is bliss, or could be.

On the other hand, if there is a way of escape for anyone, then surely everyone ought to be told about it. And there is! It may be narrow and only discovered by the few (Matt 7:14); but it is open to all. There is no need for any human being to spend the rest of their existence in that ghastly place. To put that more positively, it is possible for any human being to spend eternity in heaven.

Two qualifications are needed for heaven: forgiveness and holiness. The one cancels our sinful past; the other prepares us for our sinless future. It is impossible for us either to forgive ourselves or to make ourselves holy. The good news is that what is impossible with man is possible with God. He is able and willing to grant both forgiveness and holiness, as free gifts of his grace, to any who repent of their sins and believe in his power to save (to the uttermost as well as from the guttermost!).

Such a statement sounds like a typical preacher's cliché. It needs careful unpacking. Salvation may be free, but it is not cheap, either for the Lord or us. For him, the cost was the death of his only Son on a cross. For us it is to take up the cross daily and follow him. Who was it said that the entrance fee is nothing but the annual subscription is everything?

54

All the divine resources are now available to us, but we need to avail ourselves of them. God has done everything possible and necessary to save us from hell – except force us to accept his remedy. We are still free to resist his Spirit and to refuse his salvation.

Four persons, three divine and one human, are involved in every escape from hell. Though all are acting together, it will be helpful to consider each of them separately.

FATHER'S AFFECTION

God created the human race because he so enjoyed his only Son that he desired to have a larger family, to bring many sons to glory. Even after those intended for such a wonderful destiny refused to be his loving and obedient children, his love for them continued to be so strong that he was willing to make a supreme sacrifice to win them back (John 3:16 is deservedly the most widely known scriptural statement of this amazing truth).

So far we have considered hell almost exclusively from a human point of view – what it would be like for us to be sent there. Few stop to think about the divine point of view – what it would be like for him to have to send us there. Three insights might help us to appreciate this.

First, God never intended hell for human beings. As we have already seen (in chapter 3), it is being 'prepared for the devil and his angels' (Matt 25:41). As 'immortal' creatures (in that, having once been made, they 'cannot die'; Luke 20:36), they will one day have to be completely isolated from God's heaven and earth. For them there cannot be any chance of escaping hell. Having once known heaven itself and rejected it, not even the blood of Jesus can do anything for them (Heb 2:16).

Second, God has no pleasure whatsoever in the death of wicked human beings; he does experience pleasure when they turn away from their wickedness and towards him (Ezek 18:23). The idea that hell gives a God of revenge the satisfaction of getting his own back on those who have insulted him could not be further from the truth. It is slanderous even to suggest it. Those who do have never even begun to understand what the word 'lost' means (the prodigal son knew perfectly well where he was – he was 'lost' only to his heart-broken father). One can only imagine God's feelings when he has to discard as 'rubbish' any who once carried his own image. That can only cause profound pain, not malicious pleasure. God is not a sadist.

Third, he has done everything he could to save us from such a fate. We have already made this point, but it cannot be repeated often enough. God is in the business of recycling rubbish, restoring fallen creatures to their original condition and purpose, salvaging the ruined, saving the lost (beautifully illustrated in the return of the slave Onesimus, which means 'Useful', to his master; Philemon 11). This is his real pleasure, the work he loves to do.

Nor did he wait for us to want to be salvaged before taking action on our behalf. The initiative is his, not ours. He loved us before we loved him. He chose to save us long before we chose to be saved. Though we were not seeking him, he came to seek (and to save) us. That is why those who are being saved know themselves to be predestined for such favour and future (it does not follow that those not saved have been predestined to failure).

God's saving grace came to us through his Son.

SON'S ATONEMENT

With his lips Jesus gave us all the information about hell we need to know, including the kind of behaviour that qualifies anyone to go there. In his life he showed us the kind of behaviour that qualifies for heaven. But what he said and what he did could only lead us to despair, as indeed they did for one of his closest companions ('Go away from me, Lord; I am a sinful man'; Luke 5:8). Those who regard Jesus simply as a good example to follow have never tried to follow his example!

It was through his death, burial and resurrection that Jesus made it possible for us to escape hell and enter heaven. Having descended into hell and ascended into heaven, he has pioneered the way, blazed a trail for us to follow (a point made in the epistle to the Hebrews; 2:10).

He descended into hell. This is not something that happened after his death (as older versions of the Apostles' Creed seem to imply; modern versions rightly change 'hell' to 'hades' or simply 'the dead', that is, the world of disembodied spirits). No, he experienced hell while still in his body, for the last three of the six hours he hung on the cross.

Hell is total darkness and from noon till three on that afternoon Jesus was in that darkness. As the star had shone brightly at his birth, the sun was now eclipsed at his death (neither event was 'natural'; both were supernatural signs, pointing to the unique significance of the two events). Hell is also a thirsty place and during this period Jesus cried out: 'I thirst'. He was offered vinegar (which would have aggravated his thirst) and wine (which he refused, having vowed not to drink it again until the kingdom had fully come). Above all, hell is a place where God cannot be found, for hell is separation from God – hence Jesus' cry of dereliction: 'My God, my God, why have you forsaken me?' (taken from Psalm 22, the whole of which is a remarkable prediction of his suffering, considering that King David, its author, had never observed crucifixion, much less experienced it).

For the first time in all eternity, the Son had lost contact with his Father, which meant also, at the human level, loss of understanding as to what was happening. In our own small way, we can identify with his perplexity; we, too, have been so overwhelmed with personal sorrow and loneliness that we have uttered an anguished 'Why?'

But we now know why he suffered so. And he himself knew why, both before and after, though not during, those dark hours. He was paying the price to liberate us from our slavery to sin, a 'ransom for many' (Mark 10:45). His death was an atoning sacrifice, the propitiation for our sins (Rom 3:25). He who knew no sin was being 'made sin' on our behalf (2 Cor 5:21). He was bearing our sins in his body on the 'tree' (1 Pet 2:24). He took our place as a condemned criminal. He was our substitute in death.

Forgiveness is now possible. It is written in his blood. The penalty has been paid, the debt cancelled. But the cross also means that unforgiven sin must now be punished – God can no longer overlook it and man can no longer excuse it (Acts 17:30; Rom 3:25). Since Calvary, the world is in a different moral relationship with its Maker, with much greater potential expression of his justice and his mercy. Both heaven and hell are now opened wide.

He ascended into heaven. God vindicated his Son. Men condemned him as worthy to die; God raised him before his body could decay. Men derided his claim to be their king; God gave him all authority on earth and in heaven. Jesus is now Lord.

He has gone to prepare a place for us. He is interceding for us. He will come back and take us to be where he is. He is in absolute control of all the forces arrayed against us, including the devil and all his demons.

In going before, he has opened up the way to heaven – and we may follow in his footsteps. But *can* we? Even with the past atoned for, our sins forgiven and our relationship with God restored, how could we ever walk the way Jesus walked, live the way he lived? Through him we have forgiveness, but where will we get holiness?

He has the answer to that, too. In the deepest sense, he *is* the answer, for he is our righteousness (1 Cor 1:30) and we can become the righteousness of God in him (2 Cor 5:21). It is an amazing exchange: he takes our sins, we take his righteousness!

In other words, Christ is a *double* substitute. He takes our place in death and in life. He dies for us and lives in us. But how is such a thing possible? How can he live in us down here on earth when he is now up there in heaven?

SPIRIT'S ASSISTANCE

Enter the third person of the Trinity. He had always existed and had been with people from time to time, anointing them with supernatural gifts and graces. He was uniquely with Jesus, from his baptism (Luke 3:21f) and temptations (Luke 4:1) to his death (Heb 9:14) and resurrection (Rom 8:11). He had been 'with' the disciples who followed Jesus, but would later be 'in' them (John 14:17).

One of the first things Jesus did after ascending to heaven was to ask his Father to send the Spirit to take his place back on earth as the 'Encourager' and 'Standby' for his disciples (both titles are better translations of the Greek word *parakletos* than the rather anaemic 'Comforter', which in English seems to have neglected its middle syllable 'fort' and its meaning of 'fortify'). As he died for them at the Jewish feast of Passover, he came to live in them (by his Spirit) at the following feast of Pentecost. He had told them they would be better off with this internal, invisible presence (always and everywhere) than they had been with his external, visible presence.

Holiness is now possible. For he is the *Holy* Spirit. Righteousness is no longer a matter of external appearance, which so easily leads to pride at best and hypocrisy at worst (as in the Pharisees); it is an internal transformation of motive and desire, leading to the right behaviour and relationships.

Holiness is the fruit of the Spirit – one fruit (singular) with nine flavours (Gal 5:22f): love, joy and peace in the Lord; patience, kindness and goodness (generosity) towards others; faithfulness, meekness and self-control in one's self. This is the very character of Jesus himself, faithfully reproduced in those who 'walk in the Spirit'. However, like all fruit, it takes time to form and ripen.

Nor is the process automatic or inevitable. Branches need to 'abide' (stay) in the vine or they do not bear any fruit (John 15:4). Believers need to 'make every effort . . . to be holy; without holiness no one will see the Lord' (Heb 12:14). We have a part to play.

BELIEVER'S ADHERENCE

Though Father, Son and Holy Spirit are working together to save us from hell, putting forgiveness and holiness within our grasp (the kingdom is 'at hand'), our active co-operation is required. Gifts need to be received – and used. Free offers need to be claimed.

Christ died for the sins of the whole world (even Calvin believed that). But it is patently obvious that the whole world is not enjoying forgiveness or experiencing holiness. What is the missing factor? The fourth person required to complete the picture – yourself!

The first name for the new faith of the disciples was 'the Way'.

It was a new way of living (and dying). It was the way to heaven. The heart of it was a personal relationship with the Jesus who said of himself: 'I am the way' (John 14:6).

But 'way' implies a road to be travelled, a journey to be completed. It is those who finish, not those who start, who reach their destination. A good ending is as essential as a good beginning. The race is won at the finishing-post, by those who press on to the goal to win the prize (Phil 3:12–14; Heb 12:1f).

The first thing is to *get on the way*. A good start is a great help, as a poor start can be a real handicap. There are four initial steps we need to take to get properly started. The first is to repent (getting off the wrong road, the broad way that leads to destruction). The second is to believe in Jesus (by trusting him to do what he says he will and obeying what he tells us to do). The third is to be baptised (submerged in water as a burial of our old life which is dead and a bath to start us off clean in the new life). The fourth is to receive the Holy Spirit – by being consciously filled to overflowing, usually through the mouth. (See my book *The Normal Christian Birth*, Hodder and Stoughton, 1989, for a much more detailed account of the four steps.)

Alas, many disciples have been 'badly birthed', missing out on one or more of these vital steps. They do not travel along the way as fast or as far as those who begin right. But it's never too late in this life to catch up on what was missed; indeed, it is urgent to do so as soon as possible. A car goes best when it's firing on all four cylinders!

Even those who have been 'properly birthed' can make the mistake of thinking they have arrived (or, at least, that they have their ticket to heaven and have boarded a train that will take them all the way). The Christian life is a walk, not a ride. To be born again is to have set off in the right direction, to begin the journey (which John Bunyan so vividly portrayed in *Pilgrim's Progress*). They have not arrived, but are 'on the Way'.

The next thing is to *keep on the way*. The Christian life is dynamic, not static. A godly life is a walk with God. For God is a God who walks and we soon lose touch if we don't keep up with him. Jesus walked with his disciples (most of his teaching and healing was 'in the way'), even to his death and after his resurrection (Luke 24:13–35);

he now walks among the lampstands (the churches; Rev 2:1) and even in heaven we will walk with him (Rev 3:4).

The New Testament is full of warnings about those who fail to arrive at their destination. The failure of the majority of Hebrew slaves who left Egypt to reach Canaan is used by three apostolic writers as a warning to believers (in 1 Cor 10, Heb 4 and Jude). Christians are in as much danger of being 'cut off' as Jews, unless they 'continue' in God's kindness (Rom 11:22). God is able to keep us from falling, provided we keep ourselves in his love (Jude 21,24).

To keep on the way is the same as to stay (abide) in Christ, which is to go on believing in him. The noun 'faith' is the same as faithfulness or fidelity, in both the Hebrew and the Greek languages. To trust someone is to keep on trusting them, come what may. The verb 'believe' (more common than the noun in the New Testament) is often in the present tense, which in Greek is called the 'present continuous' tense, because it refers to a continual action, to *go on* doing something or to be *presently* doing it. What a difference this makes to some familiar and favourite texts: 'For God so loved the world that he gave his one and only Son, that whoever goes on believing (or, is presently believing) in him shall not perish but go on having (or, is presently having) eternal life' (John 3:16; the same tense is used in 20:31).

Those who do not hold firmly to the word have believed in vain (1 Cor 15:2). It is possible to shipwreck faith (1 Tim 1:19). We must be the more eager to make our calling and election sure (2 Pet 1:10; note that it is *we* who make it sure). Those who overcome will not have their names blotted out of the Lamb's book of life (Rev 3:5; the implication for those who fail to overcome is clear). Those who endure to the end will be saved (Mark 13:13). The letter to the Hebrews is packed with appeals to 'go on' and warnings about the consequences of 'going back' (2:1–3; 3:6,12–14; 6:4–11; 10:23–27; 12:3,14). Branches that do not abide in the vine are finally 'thrown in the fire and burned' (John 15:6).

Such a line of teaching usually provokes two questions, even objections. First, does this not teach salvation by works, that we save ourselves by our own efforts? Second, does it not destroy assurance, our inner certainty that we are going to heaven?

The first is raised by those who emphasise the sovereignty of God. Salvation, as they say, depends entirely on his election of the individual. This predestinating grace cannot be resisted and will inevitably result in repentance and faith, guaranteeing the perseverance of the saint and certain arrival in heaven. It follows that, since only some are elected, God does not want all men to be saved; nor did Christ die for all men, but only for the elect, since it is inconceivable that his atonement would fail to accomplish its purpose. Ironically, those who hold this scheme of things (generally referred to as 'Calvinist' or 'Reformed') are those who have held on most faithfully to the traditional understanding of hell, while denying that it has any relevance whatever to the elect believer. Their motivation is laudable – they seek to exalt the grace and mercy of God by denying to fallen man in his pride any thought of making a contribution to his own salvation. All is of God from beginning to end, even the decision that leads to salvation; we can only worship the mercy that chose to save some sinners, despite themselves. Any suggestion that salvation depends on *our* continued faith, or even *our* initial step of faith, is anathema, transferring glory from God to man.

What can we say to this? In a word – *co-operation is not contribution.* A ship's passenger falls overboard. A crew member throws him a rope, shouting, 'Get hold of this'. When the drowning man does, he calls again, 'Now hold on till I get you back to the ship'. The man is saved. Who by? Will the passenger ever claim to have saved himself? Will he be proud of his 'contribution' to his rescue? Or will he be so full of gratitude to his rescuer that such thoughts would never even occur to him? If he was saved by works, it was by the works of his rescuer; his own actions were actions of faith in that rescuer. In no sense would he regard his actions as earning, deserving or even 'worthy of' his salvation. They were the desperate actions of a man who could not possibly save himself and put all his trust in someone else.

Faith is active, not passive. It is a gift of God, but the gift can be refused or received and exercised. Faith without action is dead, it cannot save (Jas 2:14,26; it is a tragedy that the word 'works' was ever used in this verse, causing an apparent contradiction with Paul, which even Luther misunderstood). This active faith is our responsible response to God's unmerited grace. We co-operate with, not contribute to, our salvation when by faith we lay hold of Christ at the beginning of the way and keep tight hold of him on the way, until he brings us safely to heaven.

For salvation is a process, which has begun but is by no means completed yet. We *have been* saved (from sin's penalty by justification), we *are being* saved (from sin's power by sanctification) and we *will be* saved (from sin's presence by glorification); all three tenses of the verb 'saved' are used in the New Testament. The process will only be complete when Jesus will appear a second time, not to bear sin, but to bring salvation to those who are waiting for him (Heb 9:28).

What, then, does this mean for the doctrine of assurance? What can we be sure of now? We can be sure we are 'being saved', that we are on 'the way' to heaven. But this assurance is not based on a syllogistic deduction from scripture (the Bible says it, I believed it, that settles it), nor on a simplistic decision for Christ (I prayed the sinner's prayer). It springs from a relationship, not just once entered into, but continuously enjoyed. As we walk with the Lord, 'the Spirit himself goes on witnessing with our spirit that we are God's children' (Rom 8:16; present continuous tense again). When we walk in the flesh rather than the Spirit, one of the first things to suffer is that witness of our Spirit. We lose our assurance.

So we can and ought to be sure that we are heading for heaven. But we can only be sure we've got there when we arrive. Billy Graham, asked by a B.B.C. interviewer what his first thought in heaven would be, instantly replied: 'Relief!' John Bunyan wrote at the end of *Pilgrim's Progress*: 'Then I saw that there was a way to Hell, even from the gates of Heaven.' Paul retained a healthy fear that, having preached to others, he should not be disqualified himself (1 Cor 9:27).

To close on a positive note, there is no need for anyone to fail. With Father, Son and Holy Spirit for us, who can be against us – except ourselves. We are saved by grace (his works, not ours) through faith, continued and persistent faith. Forgiveness is given to those who go on believing (and go on repenting and confessing; 1 John 1:9). Holiness is given to those who go on believing (as we continue to trust and obey, he is able to complete the good work he has begun in us; Phil 1:6). All things are ours in Christ (1 Cor 3:21–23). His divine power has given us everything we need for life and godliness (2 Pet 1:3); it's up to us to make our calling and election sure (2 Pet 1:10).

If any human beings find themselves in hell, they will have no one but themselves to blame. If any find themselves in heaven, they will have no one but the Lord to praise.

6   THE REVERSE

There are only two future destinies open to the whole human race – heaven or hell. Every human being will finish up in one place or the other. They could not be more different; they are exact opposites. What may be said positively about heaven may be said negatively about hell – and vice-versa. One place is as good as the other is bad.

Heaven is the reverse of hell. The light of heaven makes the darkness of hell seem all the blacker. The communion with God in heaven makes separation from God in hell all the more terrible. The golden streets of heaven contrast sharply with the rotting rubbish in hell.

This chapter is about heaven. Its inclusion is not just to highlight the horror and misery of hell. Those who go there will be fully aware of what they have missed; the knowledge of heaven will be part of their anguish (cf. Matt 8:11f). No wonder there will be 'weeping and gnashing of teeth'.

The main reason is that the desire to escape hell is essentially a negative motive and needs to be reinforced by the positive desire to enter heaven. Only when the two are blended in balance is there a genuine understanding of the need for the 'full' gospel, which includes sanctification as well as justification, holiness as well as forgiveness – both of which are free gifts of divine grace to those who live by faith.

Hell may be disputed, for obvious reasons, even among believers. Heaven is rarely argued about, again for obvious reasons, except among unbelievers. Two criticisms have been levelled against the church's teaching on heaven.

Some say it is a *harmless delusion*. The product of human imagination, it is a self-induced compensation for the discomforts

65

and difficulties of life as we know it. Pearly gates and golden streets belong to the realm of fairy tales (what's so different between fairies and angels, anyway?).

So jokes are told about heaven (usually involving problems of admission by St Peter), expressing the teller's doubts about the whole idea. Another form of disguised scepticism is the 'awkward' question, which assumes that belief in heaven is ridiculous. Such was the Sadducees' 'problem' about the woman widowed seven times after seven childless marriages (statistically an unlikely event, to say the least!). Which husband would claim her in heaven? Jesus corrected their false assumption that earthly relationships still apply, but rebuked them sharply for their underlying disbelief in bodily existence beyond the grave, which was the real thought behind their conundrum (Luke 20:27–38).

Others regard heaven as a *dangerous distraction*. It savours of escapism, inducing contentment with injustice here by promising compensation hereafter ('negro' spiritual songs sung by slaves on American cotton plantations are often cited as examples). It was Charles Kingsley (the Anglican clergyman who wrote *Tom and the Water Babies*) who first used the phrase 'opiate of the people' for other-worldly religion. Karl Marx was quick to pick up the charge, though he changed the wording to 'opium'. This insinuation is embodied in the popular jibe that heaven is just 'pie in the sky when you die' (I always want to reply that that's better than 'pain in the pit when you flit'!).

So the world has increasingly criticised the church for being 'so heavenly minded that she is no earthly use'. Alas, the church has been so sensitive to this accusation that she has swung to the opposite extreme. Eager to comment on social and political issues of the day, preachers seem reluctant to talk about the world to come. Preaching about heaven has declined simultaneously with preaching about hell.

Yet eternity is a good deal longer than time. Life here is brief and soon over. If we really believed that we are just pilgrims passing through, preparing for a far longer existence somewhere else, we would surely make it our primary task to remind others of that future, make sure they were heading for the right destination and help them on their journey towards it. We would be talking much more about heaven. What would we be saying?

'Heaven' has different meanings in scripture. The lowest refers to the atmosphere around the earth, in which the birds and insects fly. The next up refers to the 'sky' beyond, in which the stars shine (what we would call 'outer space'). Hebrew thought conceived many 'layers' (Paul visited the 'third heaven', in what was probably an 'out-of-the-body experience'). 'Highest heaven' was God's dwelling-place, above all his creation.

The distance between heaven and earth is a key to the biblical teaching on heaven. It is relative, since it is measured in spiritual rather than physical terms. At the creation they are so close that the 'Most High' God can take an evening stroll in the garden of Eden (Gen 3:8). But the rebellious 'fall' of man (and woman) creates a great gulf, which underlies the rest of the Old Testament. God seems distant, a long way off. To speak to him, one must 'call'; worship must be a joyful noise! Jacob's dream of a long ladder stretching all the way from earth to heaven is typical and explains why angels are so prominent in the Old Testament – they act as mediating messengers; even the law of Moses was delivered by angels (Heb 2:2).

The change in the New Testament is striking. In the person of Jesus, heaven touches earth again. The kingdom of heaven is 'at hand' (within reach). One of the most startling statements Jesus ever made was: 'No one has ever gone into heaven except the one who came from heaven, *who is in heaven*' (John 3:13; emphasis mine). So he didn't leave heaven to come here; he brought it with him!

We have already seen that most of our information about hell is found on the lips of Jesus; the same goes for heaven, too. Ultimately, it is his testimony we have to trust – all of it (including what his Spirit says to the churches in the book of Revelation). Jesus was aware of human scepticism about his knowledge: 'If I have told you earthly things and you do not believe, how can you believe if I tell you heavenly things?' (John 3:12). He claimed that he would never have raised false hopes in such an important matter: 'In my Father's house are many rooms; if it were not so, I would have told you' (John 14:2). When he ascended into heaven, he was simply going back home. Heaven was, and is, where he really belongs.

It is also where those who believe in him really belong. There is a real sense in which heaven is already our home. Those who have been crucified, buried and raised with him (Gal 2:20; Rom 6:4) have also ascended with him and are even now seated with him in heavenly places (Eph 2:6). Though our physical senses tell us only too frequently and forcefully that we are still down here on earth, our real 'life is now hidden with Christ in God' (Col 3:3).

When the body dies, our total consciousness will be that of the spirit and therefore only of those heavenly places in which we have been already blessed (Eph 1:3). We shall then truly be 'away from the body and at home with the Lord' (2 Cor 5:8). Though disembodied (Paul calls it being 'unclothed'), such a state is nevertheless 'better by far' (Phil 1:23).

Having said this, it is probably misleading to describe this transition as 'going to heaven', as it often is. Strictly speaking, heaven is a 'place' for embodied spirits and therefore belongs to that third phase of our existence which lies beyond Jesus' second coming, the general resurrection and the Day of Judgement. 'And if I go and prepare a place for you, I will come back and take you to be with me that you also may be where I am' (John 14:3). So what will that 'place' be like?

RENEWED COSMOS

God's purpose in redemption is much greater than getting people into heaven. He intends to redeem all his creation, not just his human creatures. He intends to 'make all *things* new' (Rev 21:5). So there is to be a new heaven and a new earth, neither of which presently exist – in fact, a whole new universe. The present universe will have 'passed away' (the phrase we usually use for death). It will be destroyed by fire (2 Pet 3:10), which perhaps means that every atom will be split, releasing its inherent energy. In that case, the world would end in a nuclear holocaust, but one triggered off by God rather than man.

It will surprise many that the earth has a future or, more correctly, that there is to be a future earth. The church has either so concentrated on heaven that it has overlooked this new earth (leaving it in the hands of some cults) or, in recent days, has so taken up the ecological concern for the old earth that the new earth is forgotten. While Christians should have a legitimate concern about the exploitation and pollution which spoil our planet, they do not share the panic of those who think that this is the only earth we shall ever have and that if we ruin this one, the human race will become extinct. The God who made this world can, and will, make another. It will be peopled by those who have a sense of responsibility to their Creator as well as for the creation (significantly, the word 'nature' is not used in scripture, much less 'Mother Nature'; goddess fertility cults are roundly condemned as idolatry).

The new earth (and heaven) will provide an environment for those with new bodies. Indeed, the whole creation is already groaning with frustration until our bodies are redeemed (Rom 8:22f). Our hope is not just of 'going to heaven' but of living in a new heaven and a new earth, around which we shall be able to move as freely as Jesus did in his ascension. The new heaven and earth will be as close to each other as they were at the dawn of creation. It is remarkable how closely the last two chapters in the Bible resemble the first two – even the tree of life reappears after its long absence (Gen 2:9; Rev 22:2).

Life will be focused, as it is now, on the city – but then on one designed and constructed by God himself and the Carpenter from Nazareth. Even Abraham knew about this project (Heb 11:10), which may explain why he was content to leave his brick-built house at the age of eighty and live in a tent for the rest of his life – a classic case of contentment here inspired by compensation hereafter!

The 'new Jerusalem' will be a vast conurbation that will house millions, yet be of 'human scale' (urban architects have wrestled with this combination, but God will have the ideal solution to the problem). The dimensions given mean that the whole city would just fit inside the moon, if it were hollow; alternatively, it would cover two-thirds of the European continent. Since the breadth, length and height are the same, its shape will be either a cube or a pyramid.

The materials from which it is built will be both pure (pure gold is white, almost transparent, rather than the yellow or green we are familiar with) and precious (what we know as gemstones). The choice of the latter is remarkable, in the light of modern scientific discoveries. The stones listed in Revelation are all extremely hard (7. or over on Mohs' scale) and all 'anisotropic' in pure light (when viewed in light refracted through a cross-polarised filter, they produce all the colours of the rainbow in an infinite variety of patterns, whatever their original colour). No stones are used which are 'isotropic' (like diamonds or rubies, which lose all colour in such light). This difference could not possibly have been known by the 'John' who wrote Revelation and is another startling proof that God inspired scripture. There is a further distinction, which may have been known then. All the stones used have a crystal shape which is more or less oblong, with sharp angles (trigonal, tetragonal or hexagonal) and are therefore easier to build together, whereas the precious stones not used are squat and rounded (the crystals are 'cubic').

Water will run through the middle of the city, a feature of many old and new cities (in both Brasilia and Canberra, valleys were dammed to create this feature). The gates will always be open, for security will be no problem. Constructed in heaven, it will be transported down to earth (so God was the first to think of building a city out in space!). Its aesthetic quality will be breathtaking – like the appearance of a bride at her wedding.

What will life be like in this megalopolis and its environs?

REDEEMED CONDITION

Life in the new heaven and earth can be described in two ways – negative (the features of our present life that will be absent) and positive (the new features that will be present). We list seven under each head, beginning with the former.

There will be *no sex*. And we won't even miss it! Jesus made it quite clear that we shall be 'like the angels, who neither marry (like men) nor are given in marriage (like women)'. Since they 'cannot die', they do not need to reproduce or provide family life to nurture the young (Luke 20:35f). So our marriage relationships are only 'until death us do part'. Blood relationships will also have dissolved.

There will be *no suffering*. Hospitals will be forgotten, doctors and nurses redundant. Handicaps and deformities will not mar our 'glorious' bodies, though scars gained in the service of the kingdom may remain as 'battle honours', as did the nailprints in the body of the Lord Jesus (John 20:27). Paul had many of these (2 Cor 11:24f; Gal 6:17).

There will be *no separation*. Life here is full of 'Goodbyes'. Distance and death are constantly interfering with our relationships. Perhaps this is why there will be 'no longer sea' (Rev 21:1); no one will 'go overseas'.

There will be *no sorrow*. One of the most beautiful statements made about our heavenly Father is that he 'will wipe away every tear from their eyes' (Rev 21:4), as if saying: 'There, there, it's all over; there's no need to cry any more'.

There will be *no shadow*. Pure light (but not from the sun) will reach every nook and cranny, and shine all the time. There will be no darkness, no night, no lamp-posts in the streets of gold.

There will be *no sanctuary*. No spires, steeples or towers of temple or church will break the skyline. All the buildings will be residential; none will be religious (no cathedral repair appeals!). God will be worshipped anywhere – and any time.

There will be *no sin*. Nothing will defile or pollute. Pride and greed, envy and jealousy, lust and lies – all such things will have disappeared. There won't even be any temptations, no forbidden fruit (the tree of knowledge of good and evil will not reappear with the tree of life). Everything there can be freely enjoyed. That will be heaven!

Even the negatives are good news; how much more the positive.

There will be *rest*. Not sitting or lying down doing nothing, but walking and working without weariness. Stimulating activity will keep us constantly refreshed; that is the essence of 'recreation'. But the root cause of the 'rest' will be the inner peace of the soul (*shalom*, the first word Jesus used after his resurrection) that is in perfect harmony with itself, its environment, its companions and its Creator.

There will be *reward*. Heaven is not to be thought of as an egalitarian socialist republic in which all are equal. There will be great differences, compensation for special faithfulness while on earth. Some will wear crowns of honour and glory. All will 'shine like stars' (Dan 12:3), but 'star differs from star in splendour' (1 Cor 15:41).

The persecuted and especially the martyred will have great rewards (Matt 5:11f).

There will be *responsibility*. We shall serve the Lord day and night (Rev 7:15); twenty-four hour shifts! What kind of work will it be? We have no idea. But we do know this, that how we do our work on earth (whatever it is, whether that of a housewife, missionary or taxi-driver) will decide how good a job we get there (the Lord is not so much interested in what job we do as how we do the job we have).

There will be *revelation*. We shall 'know fully, even as we have been fully known' (1 Cor 13:12). The God who knows how many hairs there are on our head (the range is from ninety to a hundred and twenty thousand depending on whether we are dark, fair or ginger) will share all his secrets with us. We shall get answers to all our theological questions (will Calvinists and Arminians find they have both been right?) and those about providence (why he allowed major disasters and personal tragedies).

There will be *recognition*. How will we know each other, especially those who died very young or very old, whose new bodies will be in their prime? The answer is: in the same way that Peter, James and John recognised Moses and Elijah on the Mount of Transfiguration, though they had never met them and they had died centuries earlier. By immediate cognition, instant realisation.

There will be *righteousness*. It will be the 'home of righteousness' (2 Pet 3:13). Positive goodness really belongs there and will be entirely 'fitting'. Heaven is the source of everything that is right. The whole character of the place will look right, feel right and be right. No moral pollution will spoil the environment. Alas, we have become so accustomed to evil that it is almost impossible to imagine a world without it. Yet it will come.

There will be *rejoicing*. If the angels throw a party when one sinner repents, what will the atmosphere be like when the saints go marching in? And how will forgiven sinners feel when they realise they're safe home at last, with all trials and troubles behind them? No wonder heaven is pictured as a celebration feast. It will be the biggest banquet ever. Jesus will drink wine again (Mark 14:25) but has chosen to be the waiter to serve the food (Luke 12:37; note that the context reminds us that the feast is for those properly dressed and ready waiting). But the best thing will not be the food or drink, but the company.

RECONCILED COMMUNITY

Heaven is best summed up in the word 'home'. But what is a home? Just a place to live? No. That's a house. What turns a house into a home? Not personal property or familiar furniture but relaxed relationships. Home is where you love and are loved.

We have sketched *what* heaven will be like, but the more important question is *who* will be there. This is the heart of heaven.

Saints will be there. The great figures of faith in the Old Testament (listed in Hebrews 11) will be there; even now they are waiting for us to join them. The New Testament apostles will be there, as will the heroes and heroines from two thousand years of church history. To meet them all will be a holy privilege. But around these known names will be a 'great multitude that no one could count, from every nation, tribe, people and language' (Rev 7:9), who have been known only to God, but will then be able to be known by us. How many new friends we shall have – and all eternity to get to know them!

Angels will be there. Thousands of them. We may well recognise some who have been in our streets, homes and even cars (if they always had wings and harps, it would be somewhat difficult to 'entertain them unawares'; Heb 13:2). When we discover how often they protected and helped us, we will probably be amazed and grateful. It will be a greater surprise to find that we will then rank above them in the created order. Though man was made a little lower than the angels (Ps 8:5), our humanity in Christ has been lifted above them (Heb 2:5-10). They will be our servants! How well they looked after Lazarus the beggar, as soon as he left this world (Luke 16:22).

Jesus will be there. What joy will be his as he sees the results of the travail of his soul – and is satisfied (Isa 53:11). And what joy will be ours to see him as he really is and to be able to thank him personally for all that he went through to make it possible for us to be there. He already has about two hundred and fifty names and titles, every one of which we shall want to use when we address him. How will he address us? Will he have a new name for each individual (Rev 2:17), describing what that person means to him? We do know that collectively he is not ashamed to call us 'brothers' (Heb 2:11). Yet, as the Holy Spirit directs attention away from himself and towards the Son, so the Son will direct attention away from himself towards the Father. He came to us so that he could bring us back to the Father. He only claimed the kingdoms of this world so that he could return them to the Father, 'so that God may be all in all' (1 Cor 15:28).

We have at last reached the climax: *God* will be there. Heaven is the Father's house, his family home. His desire to have a larger family will at last be fulfilled. And we shall see him face to face; no longer through the dim reflection of a mirror (1 Cor 13:12). This was the intimate communion which his only Son had always enjoyed (John 1:1 literally says that 'the Word was face to face with God'). Now reconciled and restored human beings will also have the same unspeakable privilege of looking into the Father's face and seeing its loving expression. Saints through all the ages have longed for and looked forward to this beatific vision. 'Blessed are the pure in heart, for they shall see God' (Matt 5:8).

Where will all this happen? The answer is the biggest surprise of all – and perhaps the most wonderful. We are not 'going to heaven' to be with God; he is coming to earth to be with us! The 'new Jerusalem' comes down out of heaven (Rev 21:10). But it is not just a new place for us to live in; it is to be God's new home as well! He is moving house, changing his address. Henceforth, he will be 'our Father, who art on earth . . .' The Bible does not say that our dwelling-place will be with him; the angel shouts in wonder: 'Behold (just look at this!), the dwelling of God is with men, and he will live with them' (Rev 21:3). The God who walked in Eden will move in with us. The new earth will be the centre of the new universe. The name 'Immanuel' ('God-with-us') will take on a whole new meaning. To have had the Son with us on earth was wonder enough; to have the Father here as well can only fill us with awed amazement.

Truly, 'no eye has seen, no ear has heard, no mind has conceived what God has prepared for those who love him' (1 Cor 2:9, quoting

Isa 64:4). But the Bible does not allow us to be carried away into unreality by the contemplation of such marvels. The same two chapters which give us most information bring us down to earth again with a bump, by reminding us that there are still human beings 'outside' all this and in the 'lake of fire' (Rev 21:8; 22:15). The joys of heaven on earth are for those who 'go on overcoming' temptations and trials; and who 'go on washing' their robes (Rev 21:7; 22:14).

So even in the context of revealing the glory to come, the Lord includes warnings about hell. To this challenge we must return for the final chapter. Why should hell also be included in our preaching and teaching, even when we are talking about heaven?

7 THE RELEVANCE

Would it make any real difference if the subject of hell were dropped altogether from our preaching and teaching? Might such an omission improve our public relations? Has its inclusion proved an unnecessary handicap?

Discussion of such questions is not entirely speculative, since the majority of churches in Europe and many in North America have already expunged hell from their creed. He would be bold who claimed that these churches have noticeably improved in quantity or quality (the evidence seems to point in the opposite direction). However, many assert a rise in mental health by the reduction, even removal, of such 'morbid fears'.

Of course, the pragmatic issue of whether to retain or reject the traditional teaching on the subject rests on the prior question of whether it is true or not. Debate about the *relevance* of hell can only be undertaken by those convinced of its *existence*.

Even if the truth of hell has been established and is accepted, there are still other questions to be asked. For example, how prominent a place ought it to have? Should it be in the foreground or background of our thinking – and our speaking?

Extreme examples abound. There are preachers who give the impression of 'nothing but' and others who cover 'everything but'. To reach a satisfactory balance requires a preliminary study of the relation between belief in hell and other matters of belief and behaviour.

Again, we shall study its effects on unbelievers and believers separately. What is the motivating influence of hell on evangelising the former and edifying the latter?

EVANGELISING UNBELIEVERS

Some may wonder why this even needs to be discussed. To them it seems so obvious that sinners need to be saved from hell and that it will help to do this by telling them they are going there. What more needs to be said? Certainly, this thinking has provided the prime motive and simple rationale for much missionary effort in the past. Men and women have gone to the ends of the earth to rescue their fellow human beings from 'a lost eternity'. Their zeal sprang from a sense of urgency. The perishing had to be rescued before they died.

The most zealous missionaries, though not always the most wise, are still motivated by this burden. They may fall into simplistic methods and cultural mistakes, but there is no questioning their enthusiasm. On the other hand, missionary strategists who consider that a more mature approach can do without such inspiration have yet to prove that this stimulates greater, or even equal, zeal.

We must nevertheless face the fact that hell did not figure prominently in the evangelistic preaching of Jesus or the apostles. They were not given to 'dangling sinners over the pit'. Nor did they use detailed descriptions of endless suffering to persuade their hearers to seek an escape from its torments. Does this, perhaps, indicate the need to *see* sinners in this danger, but not necessarily to *tell* them? Is hell to motivate the evangelist rather than the evangelised?

It's not quite as simple as that. For one thing, Jesus and the apostles did talk freely about a future judgement and this was an integral feature in their gospel preaching. Judgement inevitably involves both reward and punishment – and it would be astonishing if there were an absence of curiosity about the nature of these. To put it another way, the gospel includes bad news about the wrath of God, as well as good news about his mercy. And this wrath, simmering in the present, would boil over in the future (John 3:36, Rom 2:5 and Rev 6:17 are just three examples of a thread running right through the New Testament). John the Baptist had begun the trend for exhorting his hearers to 'flee from the coming wrath' (Luke 3:7).

Since the first preachers were addressing Jews, it could be assumed that they already understood and believed in the concept of hell.

THE ROAD TO HELL

We have already noted that the use of 'Gehenna' as a metaphor for hell may not have been original to Jesus. The Pharisees certainly believed in it, though not, of course, for themselves (Sadducees did not believe in the future life at all, which is why they were sad, you see!). Nor was hell an unknown idea in the Gentile world. One Greek name for it (*tartarus*) is picked up in the New Testament (2 Pet 2:4).

So maybe little was said about hell because little needed to be said. But this borders on an 'argument from silence', which can be used both ways (if a thing is not mentioned this can mean everybody believed it or nobody believed it!). What is clear is that the theme of judgement was consistently included, which by implication clearly includes punishment.

Let us probe a little deeper. How essential is hell to the gospel, even if it is not prominent? One nineteenth-century theologian went so far as to say, 'Reject what the Bible tells us about hell, and we can have no understanding of the glorious gospel of the blessed God' (W.C.T. Stead, in *Dogmatic Theology*, 1871). Many twentieth-century theologians would disagree. Are they right or was he?

Hell underlines the seriousness of *sin*. It is virtually impossible for sinful man to appreciate how offensive his sin is to a holy God or how heinous is his rebellion against heaven's rule. If hell is what sin deserves, then it must be taken far more seriously than we are prone to take it. All sins are 'mortal', a matter of life and death.

This in turn will affect our view of the *atonement*. How necessary was Christ's death on the cross? What did it actually achieve? A belief in hell inclines the mind to accept 'objective' theories which see atonement in terms of satisfaction (he paid the penalty of sin to satisfy divine justice) and substitution (he took our place of guilt and shame). Disbelief in hell tends to view the cross in a more 'subjective' light as an exhibition (of God's love) or an example (of paying the supreme price for what is right); atonement is spelt 'at-one-ment' and is used to indicate reconciliation rather than compensation. Of course, there are exceptions to this generalisation and some truth in all the theories – but it remains true that the cross is viewed rather differently in the light (or rather, darkness) of hell.

Above all, our understanding of *God* himself is profoundly affected by our attitude to hell. Those who cannot believe he would ever throw anyone into hell (even a hell that annihilates rather than torments) will ultimately have a picture of God that is more sentimental than scriptural, an image born out of their own thinking rather than the God who really is and has revealed himself in Jesus. The 'loving Father' (which he is) will tend to crowd out the 'sovereign King' and the 'impartial Judge' (which he also is). This 'reductionist' theology cannot do justice to the New Testament data, never mind the whole Bible.

It is significant that those who no longer preach hell are usually strangely mute about future judgement – and even seem less certain about heaven, which may not be a coincidence (there has been a general swing from preaching about the next world to commenting on this one). Not unrelated is the definition of guilt in psychological rather than moral terms, needing therapy rather than forgiveness and certainly not deserving punishment.

Many today would question whether 'every mouth may be silenced and the whole world held accountable to God' (Rom 3:19). If all religions, sincerely and devoutly practised, are different ways to God and if all human beings are innocent until they reject the gospel and if they cannot reject it until they have received a complete, even perfect, presentation of it – then truly the missionary motive of saving the guilty from hell is an obsolete anachronism, the sooner got rid of, the better. But if, as Paul argues, 'Jews and Gentiles are alike under sin', backing this conclusion with previous revelation ('As it is written: There is no one righteous, not even one; there is no one who understands, no one who seeks God'; Rom 3:9f) – then the motive remains valid.

But what about *preaching* hell? Granted that it can and should motivate the preacher, should it be used to motivate the hearer to respond? Many would agree with the saintly Richard Baxter of Kidderminster that: 'Affrighting men will not renew their natures and kindle in them a love to God and holiness.' But he was also honest enough to admit that out of his six hundred church members, he only knew of two who had not been led to their salvation by their conviction of eternal danger. Dr Isaac Watts went one further (quite literally!) when he said that in his entire ministry he had only known one person who was not 'awakened' by such fear.

Voices of protest are not lacking, whose altruistic outlook is very critical of any 'appeal to self-interest'. They quote the hymn of Francis Xavier (1506-52):

> My God, I love Thee not because
> I hope for heaven thereby,
> Nor yet because who love Thee not
> Are lost eternally.

However, this is the devotion of a mature saint, not a desperate sinner calling on the Lord to be saved. Is it self-interest that prompts a drowning man to grab the rope thrown to him? Of course it is. Should he pause to examine his motives before grabbing it (Am I doing this for the sake of my family, mankind or just myself? Should I be doing it to please the one who has thrown the rope to me?)? Is it even possible to realise the need for salvation without any self-interest? Was not Jesus appealing to self-interest with his invitation to: 'Come to me, all you who are weary and burdened, and I will give you rest' (Matt 11:28)? Could anyone mention hell without appealing to self-interest? Or heaven, for that matter?

Let it be freely admitted that hell can be, and has been, preached in the wrong way. Two abuses have caused unnecessary offence.

Some have used their imagination to go well beyond the constraints of scripture, painting lurid and sensational pictures of the torments suffered. This unwarranted exaggeration has sometimes transformed a healthy fear (which leads to appropriate action) into an unhealthy phobia (which paralyses). Jesus certainly viewed hell with the utmost horror, to be avoided at any cost; but he never sought to manipulate his hearers' emotions by amplifying their fears with detailed descriptions. We may be thankful that an increasing number are following his example and refraining from the former excess.

A more subtle offence is given when hell is preached by those who obviously have no fear of it themselves. Popular resentment towards this attitude may be summed up in the once popular cliché: 'Blow you, Jack, I'm alright'. When sinners are told they are heading for hell by those who are sure they are heading for heaven, a negative reaction is not unexpected, since the message appears to carry overtones of arrogance. Hopefully, the emphasis of this book on the fact that most of Jesus' warnings about hell were given to his own disciples (which appears to have been overlooked or ignored by every other writer this author has studied!) will begin to correct this attitude. Perhaps the horror of hell can only be properly communicated by those who are aware of their own risk, with a humility that is readily apparent to the audience (the sinless Jesus would, of course, be an exception to this observation). The doctrine of hell can be safely handled by those who have an existential respect for it, those who preach to themselves as well as others, those who 'knowing the terror of the Lord, seek to persuade men' (2 Cor 5:11).

From one point of view, hell is good news. It assures us that God is not indifferent to evil. The mixture of good and evil in our world will not be allowed to continue indefinitely. The wicked will be judged, discarded, isolated. This is a moral universe. But this is bad news, very bad news, for all who enjoy their wickedness and cling to evil so that it becomes part of their personality – and God can only clear out the sin by throwing out the sinner. If a sinner is not willing to be separated from his sins, he will perish with them.

So hell must be preached as part of the 'whole counsel of God' (Acts 20:27), but in a proper balance with all the other parts. And the manner must be right, as well as the message – in fear and with tears. Since God has no pleasure in the death of the wicked, no preacher dare indulge in the sadistic pleasure of gloating over the destiny of enemies of the gospel.

It is safer for the evangelist to have hell more frequently in his heart than on his lips. This will fuel his fervency, increase the urgency of his appeal. Was it not General Booth who said that if he could, he would include fifteen minutes in hell in the training of all Salvation Army officers? He knew that would keep their priorities right, as well as ensure their devotion to the main objective.

We are already moving from the place of hell in preaching to unbelievers to its application in teaching believers. So let us now take that step.

EDIFYING BELIEVERS

Judging by our Lord's example, it is more important to remind saints about hell than sinners! We recall again that key text in which Jesus told his apostles, as he sent them out on their mission, to 'fear him who can destroy (ruin) both soul and body in hell' (Matt 10:28; see Scripture Study A for the interpretation of 'him' as referring to God, rather than the devil).

Here is the clue: the *fear* of the Lord. In the Old Testament, this is the 'beginning of knowledge' (Prov 1:7). It is just as much a motive for right living in the New. We are to 'work out our salvation with fear and trembling' (Phil 2:12). There are constant exhortations to fear God (e.g. 1 Pet 2:17; Rev 14:7).

To translate 'fear' as 'reverence' is to misunderstand its meaning and reduce its impact. It is much more than respect for what God *is*. It is the fear of failing to enter into what he has promised us (Heb 4:1). It is the fear of final rejection by him and separation from him. It is fear of what God can and will *do*.

The fear of God and the fear of hell are closely linked, though not identical. It is rare for the former to survive the loss of the latter. Maybe we will one day attain that 'perfect' love which casts out fear, even in this life; but until we do a blend of fear and love is both possible and necessary. There are five benefits for the believer from a healthy fear of hell.

1. *Diligence in evangelism*. This has already been discussed in the previous section. The task of evangelism is to 'rescue the perishing, care for the dying, snatch them in pity from sin and the grave' (as the old hymn puts it). If death is final and hell is permanent, the task is urgent.

Jesus left us many commands, but the last he gave (mentioned in all four gospels between the resurrection and ascension) was to make disciples of all nations, preach the gospel to every creature, offer repentance and forgiveness – sent into the world as the Father sent the Son, with compassion to seek and to save the lost. Zeal for the task tends to flag when the full meaning of the word 'lost' is itself lost.

One of the largest 'ticker-tape' parades ever held in New York was for the fire service of that city. Ahead of the uniformed firemen and their trucks marched hundreds of citizens in civilian clothes – all of whom had been saved from a horrible death by the firemen. God grant it may be the same when 'the saints go marching in'.

2. *Reverence in worship*. One New Testament writer makes the

following appeal: 'Let us be thankful, and so worship God acceptably with reverence and awe, for our God is a consuming fire' (Heb 12:28f, quoting Deut 4:24 and 9:3). Two dimensions of true worship are mentioned here, which are often missing from contemporary services and meetings.

The first is *awe*. There is much familiarity, but little fear, in many acts of praise today. There is little sense of standing on the crater edge of an active volcano when we come into the presence of the Almighty. Have we forgotten how easily he could destroy our bodies and souls in the inferno? Even the 'Quakers', given the nickname because they trembled in his presence, now prefer to be called the 'Society of Friends'.

The second is *gratitude*. It is common to thank the Lord for our blessings, both those we share with unbelievers and those we enjoy as believers. But the deepest note of gratitude comes when we recall what would have been our inevitable destination had Jesus not been willing to experience hell on the cross for us. The Lord's Supper is more likely to be the central act of worship when it is a heart-felt expression of thanks (*eucharisto* is the Greek word for 'Thank-you') for his 'descent into hell'.

3. *Perseverance in service.* The fate of those who failed to keep their lamps trimmed, to use their talents or to minister to the Lord's 'brethren' is a sobering reminder of our responsibilities.

Faith is exercised in and demonstrated by faithfulness (as we have already noted, the two English words are the same Hebrew and Greek words). The just shall live by keeping faith (Heb 2:4; note how this verse is used by New Testament writers to emphasise persistent trust and obedience in Rom 1:17 and Heb 11:38f).

This is not salvation by works, but salvation by continual faith, a faith that works through love (Gal 5:6), both love for the Lord and love for others. Jesus made the keeping of his commandments the authentication of love (John 14:21; 15:10).

4. *Obedience in holiness.* A belief in hell deepens an understanding of divine holiness and reinforces the need for holiness in his people (Lev 11:44f; 1 Pet 1:16; also Eph 1:4; 1 Thess 4:7). Centuries ago, a British layman pleaded with God's people: 'Let us then strive with all the powers at our command to overcome our habits of sin and dip ourselves deep in activities of holiness and righteousness, that

we may not undergo the sufferings of the damned but enjoy the blessed state together with the righteous.' His words are a powerful paraphrase of a verse in the New Testament already quoted more than once in these pages: 'Make every effort to be holy; without holiness no one will see the Lord' (Heb 12.14) – yet it must be admitted that Augustine persuaded the authorities of the Roman church to brand the author of these words (Pelagius) as a heretic (he did get some other things seriously wrong!).

The heart of the question is this: is sanctification as well as justification necessary to escape hell and enter heaven? Or is holiness a kind of optional extra that qualifies for added blessing here and extra reward hereafter? Was the hymn-writer correct to say that:

> He died that we might be forgiven,
> *He died to make us good*;
> That we might go at last to heaven,
> Saved by his precious blood.

The way some preach and practise the Christian life, one could amend that second line to read:

> Not needing to be good.

But we need both to be forgiven and to be made good if we are to go at last to heaven. This would be crystal clear from our Lord's teaching in the Sermon on the Mount alone, even if no other scripture made the same point. We are saved *from* sin, but *for* righteousness. The full gospel offers both. Jesus is the Lamb of God who takes away the sins of the world and baptises in the *Holy* Spirit (John 1:29,33).

Too many want one without the other, forgiveness without holiness. They hope to pass from justification to glorification, without passing through the second stage of sanctification. This is to take advantage of divine mercy. The Lord says to each one of us: 'Neither do I condemn you; go now and leave your life of sin' (John 8:11).

5. *Confidence in persecution.* When the Lord sent out his disciples two by two, he expected them to encounter hostility, suffer persecution and even face martyrdom. They could be compromised through fear for their lives.

Psychologists confirm that lesser fears can be overcome by a greater fear. This was Jesus' counsel, indeed command, to them. They were to fear God more than man, hell more than death. To fear him who can destroy body and soul in hell would cure them of fearing anyone or anything else. It would be far, far worse to lose eternal life than temporal life.

So fear of hell will literally 'en-courage' believers when they are under pressure. It will put present suffering in true perspective. It is 'not worth comparing with the glory that will be revealed' (Rom 8:18). To avoid suffering by compromise is simply not worth it. Those who deny Christ now are running the appalling risk of being disowned by him later (Matt 10:33; 2 Tim 2:12). To throw away a future inheritance for the sake of present relief can mean irrevocable loss, as Esau discovered, to his everlasting regret (Heb 12:16f; note this follows v.14).

Polycarp, one of the early Christian martyrs, refused to deny Christ when threatened with wild beasts in the arena. The frustrated Roman proconsul increased the pressure: 'I will have you consumed with fire, if you despise wild beasts, unless you change your mind.' Polycarp responded with: 'You threaten fire which burns for an hour and is soon quenched; for you are ignorant of the fire of the coming judgement and eternal punishment reserved for the wicked.'

*   *   *

So preaching hell has a place in evangelising unbelievers and teaching hell has a place in edifying believers. Conversely, its absence can seriously weaken the urgency of both ministries. The doctrine has a dual role to play in the church's twofold call to fishing and shepherding.

One parable of Jesus combines the two emphases – that of the great feast (Matt 22:1–14; see Scripture Study B for a detailed exegesis and comparison with the version in Luke). A king prepares a wedding reception for his son. When it is ready, the guests are informed, but find other things to do. This insult enrages the king, who sends his army to destroy them and their city. Determined to fill every seat at the table, he sends his servants out to persuade others to attend.

So far, the story is a warning that it is insufficient to receive, or even accept, the invitation – the vital thing is to come when called.

Then comes the shock. Most guests have come in their best clothes, but one has not bothered to change. This further insult to the king and his son is unforgivable (the man's silence shows that he had no excuse and could have put on better clothes). Attendants tie him hand and foot and throw him out into the 'darkness, where there will be weeping and gnashing of teeth' (Jesus' standard description of hell). The parable has now become a warning to those who accept the invitation, come when called, but do nothing to make themselves presentable or worthy of the occasion. It is very significant that this last incident is not mentioned in Luke's version (a gospel written for unbelievers), but in Matthew (a gospel written for believers).

The parable concludes with a summary of the whole situation: 'Many are (originally) called, but few are (finally) chosen'. In theological terms, many want to be justified, few want to be sanctified. Many want forgiveness, few want holiness. Many want to attend the heavenly banquet, few want to prepare themselves. For in real life, it is not just one who fails to dress properly, but many. Those who really understand the invitation and its purpose will want to make every effort to grace the occasion. They are not simply looking forward to the food, but to fellowship with the king and his son.

In other words, some who respond to the gospel invitation do so simply to escape the torment of hell and enjoy the delights of heaven. They do nothing to get ready and expect to be admitted to glory just as they are. They are in for a shock.

Others, perhaps a minority ('few'), know they are being invited to attend a royal occasion and look forward to an intimate relationship with the royal family in their palace. With whatever time they have, they do everything possible to make themselves ready for such a privilege. Such will 'receive a rich welcome into the eternal kingdom of our Lord and Saviour Jesus Christ' (2 Pet 1:11; note the context in vv.5–10).

Our ascended Lord has given his church evangelists to persuade lost sinners to come when called – and pastors to help them get ready for the banquet. Let both pursue their holy calling with untiring zeal, knowing that they are not just providing guests for the wedding, but actually preparing the bride herself (John 3:29; Eph 5:25f).

And let those who come under their ministries so respect their motive and receive their message that they may be found seated at the King's table. For those who do not, it would be better at the last if they had never been born.

'O God, our Father, I pray that in your great mercy every reader of this book and its unworthy author may at the last receive a rich welcome into your heavenly home – justified by your grace, sanctified by your Spirit and glorified in your presence, through the blood and in the name of your only Son Jesus Christ, our Saviour and Lord, Amen.'

SCRIPTURE STUDIES

SCRIPTURE STUDIES:
INTRODUCTION

Frequent references to chapter and verse can foster an impression that a book is thoroughly biblical, which may or may not be the case. A text out of context is a pretext!

The following ten studies look at a number of relevant passages in much greater detail than was possible or advisable in the main body of this book. Where necessary, considerable attention is given to the wider context, sometimes the character and purpose of the whole book in which the passage occurs.

It is a mixed selection, some being of more direct relevance than others. There has been a deliberate choice of a few which are normally ignored because their meaning is obscure or unacceptable. Those who believe that all scripture is inspired and profitable need to demonstrate this by tackling those parts which others avoid.

Extended exegesis has enabled some peripheral topics to be introduced. The 'millennium' is a case in point. Readers would probably want to know what eschatological position the author holds, though it must be pointed out that this does not affect the conclusions reached on the subject of hell.

The balance of biblical writers (four passages are from Matthew, two from Luke, two from Peter and one each from Paul, John and Jude) reflects the proportion of material in their writings. The fact that most of it appears in the first gospel has rarely been given its full significance, namely, that most teaching and warnings about hell were given to disciples rather than sinners.

This discovery, which is fundamental to the thesis of this book, leads straight into a major theological controversy. It is ironic that Calvinists, who have probably been the most faithful in believing and preaching the doctrine of hell, will probably dismiss this study as Arminian heresy, or even worse (since there is a quotation from Pelagius, which will not be excused by another from Augustine!).

The so-called 'five points' of Calvinism – total depravity, unconditional election, limited atonement, irresistible grace, perseverance or, more accurately, preservation of the saints (easily memorised with the mnemonic TULIP) – form an integrated 'system'. Challenge one and the whole is threatened. To suggest that the believer could risk losing his place in heaven and finding himself in hell is to question the fifth tenet, but by the same token it is implied that grace can be resisted, atonement was unlimited in its scope, election is conditional on faith and the totally depraved can respond to prevenient grace.

While this book is not intended to discuss or weigh the respective merits of 'Calvinist' and 'Arminian' theologies, I have felt bound to indicate those passages whose plain and simple meaning is at variance with the former outlook. This is particularly the case when considering the context of Jesus' warnings. Perhaps my efforts will stimulate someone of that persuasion to the pioneer endeavour of offering a 'Calvinist' explanation as to why most of these warnings were given to the first disciples and recorded in a gospel intended for the instruction of subsequent generations of Jesus' followers.

It is impossible to avoid theological issues when seeking to expound the Bible, but controversy can be healthy if it drives us back to re-examine both what the Word of God actually says and the presuppositions of our traditional interpretation of it. Personally, I do not think that any theological 'system' – Calvinist or Arminian, Augustinian or Pelagian, Reformed or Radical – is large enough or flexible enough to contain the whole counsel of God or cope with the many paradoxes of scripture.

I hope these studies will provoke the reader to have an open Bible alongside this book, checking the latter by the former. It is very foolish to read books about the Bible without direct reference to it. It is very wise to search the scriptures to see whether what is being taught is really there (as Paul's Berean audience did 'with great eagerness', Acts 17:11). I would go further and say that if my readers cannot find in these passages what I have found, I would urge them to forget what I say before they are distracted, or even damaged.

Preachers and teachers have been very much in my mind. I want to encourage them to expound whole passages rather than speak on texts (one verse, occasionally out of context) or topics (many verses, frequently out of context). The challenge of getting to grips with the flow of thought in a biblical book is immensely satisfying and infinitely rewarding. Few things build up congregational expectancy like this larger insight, provided the exposition is real (reliving the past experience of God) and *relevant* (relocating it in the present experience of man).

The Bible then becomes a self-interpreting as well as a self-authenticating book. The same Spirit of truth who inspired the writers is now available to instruct the readers (1 John 2:27). All that is required of us is an objective mind, an open heart and an obedient will.

SCRIPTURE STUDY A:
THE MORTAL FEAR

Read Matt 10:28 and Luke 12:4-5.

The message is clear – there is a 'fate worse than death'. Therefore there is a fear that is greater than the fear of death. This deeper dread is the cure for cowardice in the face of the enemy.

But there are still questions to be answered. *What* exactly is this terrible peril? *Who* is 'the one' who can threaten with it? *Why* is the warning necessary? *When* was it given?

Context, as usual, provides the clue. Jesus said the same thing twice: once when he sent the 'twelve' out on a mission and again later after the 'seventy' had returned from a later mission. On both occasions he was totally honest with them about the increasing hostility and impending danger they would face.

Hatred in their hearers would lead to rejection by the people, flogging by religious authorities, prosecution by the civil authorities, even betrayal by their own families. They would suffer assorted abuse and attempted assassination.

All this might not happen at first, but Jesus is clearly taking a long-term rather than a short-term view. Though he commands them not to go to the Gentiles now (Matt 10:5), he anticipates that they will later (Matt 10:18). His counsel is therefore relevant to all subsequent missions in his name, throughout this present age.

Fear of man is a major handicap to apostles. They must be proof against intimidation. Three times he tells them they must not be afraid (Matt 10:26,28,31). But how can they overcome such fear?

They must remember that all hidden hostility will one day be exposed and punished (Matt 10:26), that their heavenly Father cares for them and watches over them (Matt 10:29-30) and that to disown

Jesus before men means to be disowned by him before God (Matt 10:32–33).

But the best antidote for any fear is a bigger fear! Aquaphobia is overcome when one's child is drowning, claustrophobia when one's child is trapped. A prophet understood this well-known psychological mechanism: 'It will be as though a man fled from a lion only to meet a bear, as though he entered his house and rested his hand on the wall only to have a snake bite him' (Amos 5:19). It is amazing how effectively one fear can conquer another. Terror cures timidity!

Self-preservation is said to be our strongest instinct, life our most precious possession and death the ultimate threat. Our mortality thus makes us vulnerable to anyone or anything with the power to kill us. Jesus came to set us free from this crippling handicap (Heb 2:15).

He did this both by teaching and example. From these a new perspective is gained, both on the quantity and quality of life. Death is neither the end of the personal existence nor the worst thing that can happen. Only those whose outlook is bounded by this life can think otherwise.

Murder can 'only' kill the body; it cannot touch the 'soul' (the 'psyche', the real person). The self continues as a conscious being. Here Jesus is affirming the survival of a disembodied 'spirit'. Human beings do not have the power to extinguish their fellows, only to bring the physical part to an end.

That is why there is something worse than death, which only kills *part* of a person and not even the most vital part. A *whole* person, body and soul, can be 'destroyed', by someone who has the power to do so.

Who is 'the one' with this power? Some commentators assume this is a reference to the devil himself. One of his names is 'Destroyer' and hell is seen as his 'domain', in which he is free to exercise his vandalistic passion against those delivered into his hands. But there are good reasons for questioning this interpretation:

1. This would be the only New Testament text exhorting people to fear the devil, rather than the Lord;
2. The devil's kingdom or rule is in this world, not the next;

3. There is no mention of Satan elsewhere in this commissioning; the immediate context is about the Father;
4. The devil is never credited with the power to 'throw into' hell (as in the Lukan version); indeed, he is himself 'thrown into' hell (Rev 20:10; see Scripture Study J).

The threat has a divine, rather than a demonic, source. It is surely God himself, the God who can destroy the man he has created (Gen 6:7) and who is himself a 'consuming fire' (Heb 12:29). Then why does Jesus refer to him as 'the one' and not 'the Father'? There would be an understandable reticence to link this affectionate term with what some theologians have called 'the strange work' of God.

However, there may be a more subtle reason for this somewhat impersonal term. Elsewhere, Jesus himself claims to be the one to judge the nations and consign the 'cursed' to hell (Matt 25:41; cf 1 Cor 5:10). In other passages he and his Father, who are 'one', act in judgement together (e.g. Acts 17:31; Rev 6:16f). So the ambiguous anonymity may be quite deliberate.

What does it mean to 'destroy body and soul'? This may seem, at first sight, a superfluous question. In English the word is virtually synonymous with 'kill' and means to be exterminated or annihilated. Many readers therefore assume that the contrast is between death, which brings part of a person to the end of its existence, and hell, which brings the whole person to the end of his existence.

But the Greek word covers a much wider spectrum, from 'terminate existence' to 'ruin beyond recovery', or even simply 'waste'. It is by no means a foregone conclusion that hell is a place where whole persons cease to exist. The change from 'kill' (the body) to 'destroy' (body and soul) may be more than a literary variation and could indicate a qualitative as well as a quantitative threat. The change in Luke's version is even clearer: from 'kill' to 'thrown into', which leaves the question of continued existence wide open.

Whether hell involves incineration or incarceration cannot be settled either way from the verse now being discussed (it has been more fully examined in chapter 3). Suffice it to say here that continued existence in a ruined condition would certainly be much more terrifying than the death of the body; conversely, it is questionable whether extermination would be.

Before moving on, it is worth noting that Jesus speaks of the destruction of a 'body' in hell *after* the death of a body. He is not referring to the putrefaction of a corpse, which takes place in the grave rather than hell and does not affect the soul at all. He is clearly anticipating a resurrected body that can be 'thrown into' hell. This raises again the speculative question as to why God would bother to give the wicked new bodies only to annihilate them immediately afterwards! His act of 're-creation' would be more understandable if the raised body were for continued existence rather than complete annihilation.

Another point is that Jesus neither describes nor defines hell on this occasion. This can only mean that his hearers were already quite familiar with the concept and needed no further explanation; he could take it for granted.

Who is in danger of this ultimate horror? Though this verse has been very widely quoted in Christian preaching, few if any have noted, or even noticed, the *recipients* of the warning. To do so would surprise some and shock others.

Jesus is not speaking to notorious sinners or even the general public, but to his own disciples (in Luke he addresses them as 'my friends'). Nor is he giving them this serious message to pass on to others, but to apply to themselves! In spite of the immediately preceding verse (Matt 10:27 commands them to make public what they hear from him in private), the wording is clearly directed to the needs of the apostles themselves rather than those to whom they are being sent.

His purpose is to give them emotional stability in themselves rather than emotional impact on others. Their fear of God will effectively neutralise their fear of man. Note that the fear is personal in both cases. It is not fear of death versus fear of hell, but fear of 'those' who can kill the body versus 'one' who can destroy body and soul. The choice is between fear of potential killers and fear of the potential destroyer. The former is cowardice and can qualify for the 'lake of fire' (Rev 21:8).

We must now face the serious implication of all this – that Jesus warned his disciples of their own danger of being thrown into hell. It is not as if this were an isolated case. As we have seen (in chapter 4), most of the Lord's warnings were given to these same followers.

The challenge cannot be ignored, yet even those who face it tend to explain it away (perhaps because it doesn't 'fit' their theology), in one of two ways.

On the one hand, the warnings are said to be '*existential*' (virtually meaning unreal in the long run). In other words, Jesus wanted to give the disciples a bit of a fright to keep them on the straight and narrow, though, of course, there was no real danger of them ever being thrown into hell (a kind of 'carrot-and-donkey' situation in reverse). But would one who claimed to tell and be the truth resort to such deception, however mild? Would fear of actual danger be overcome by fear of something that was purely hypothetical? The suggestion is incongruous, if not absurd.

On the other hand, the warnings are said to be '*transitional*', since they were given before Jesus' death, resurrection, ascension and imparting of the Spirit – and therefore before the disciples were fully 'Christian'. But they had already received Jesus, believed in his name and been 'born of God' (if John 1:12–13 applies to anyone, it surely applies to them). And we have already noted that Matthew 10 is intended for the later and wider mission of the church to the Gentile world. Further, most of Jesus' warnings about hell relate to his second coming rather than his first.

The warning should be taken at its face value. Hell is a real danger, even for the disciples and friends of Jesus. An awareness of this risk is an essential ingredient in that fear of the Lord which is the beginning of wisdom. It is also an invaluable aid when facing human hostility and personal danger.

Jesus was an example as well as an exponent of this truth. He showed not a trace of fear when facing his executioners. Yet he experienced extreme apprehension (causing blood to ooze through the pores of his forehead) when he contemplated that separation from God, that 'descent into hell' (see chapter 5) which for him preceded, rather than followed, the killing of his body – and was for the sins of others rather than his own.

SCRIPTURE STUDY B:
THE WEDDING BANQUET

Read Matt 22:1–14 and Luke 14:15–24.

Like all the recorded parables of Jesus, this one needs to be interpreted in two contexts – the original spoken one (Jesus' hearers) and the later written one (Matthew's readers). The former reveals its meaning for yesterday and the latter its message for today.

We begin by asking when, where and why Jesus told the original 'story'. The when and where are complicated by the fact that Matthew and Luke both record it – in differing times and places (though not too far removed from each other in either). Some scholars think that the two gospel writers have used 'poetic licence' to adapt one occasion for two purposes. It is more likely that Jesus himself adapted the story for two occasions.

The first (in Luke) was on the way up to Jerusalem for the last time and at a sabbath meal in the home of a prominent Pharisee. Jesus criticised his hosts for three things – their silent hostility to his healing a case of dropsy on the Sabbath, their unseemly scramble for places at the top table and their ulterior motives in the selection of guests (those who could and would repay their hospitality). Had they invited those unable to reciprocate (the poor and helpless), they would be really blessed; they would be repaid by God rather than man and in the next world rather than this. Such hospitality would be a much better long-term investment.

In the embarrassed silence which ensued, one guest tried to redeem the situation with a pious platitude apparently agreeing with Jesus' observation, while covering his host's embarrassment. 'Blessed is the man who will eat at the feast in the kingdom of God' (clearly implying that he expected himself to be there!). Indeed, it was widely if grudgingly acknowledged that if anyone deserved to be there it was the Pharisees, who had worked hardest for it.

It was in response to this complacency that Jesus told the parable of the great feast and the invited guests who, when the time came, found excuses for not attending and were replaced by the undeserving and the unexpecting.

The story is in total accord with ancient custom: guests were given advance notice of an intended banquet, but not the specific date or time. When these details were sent later, it was assumed that the invitees would give the occasion priority over all other commitments. To accept the first invitation and decline the second would be a profound insult to the host, relegating him to secondary significance.

In this case, the host is understandably angry and determined not to waste the prepared food. His servants first search the town for potential replacements, who had neither thought nor hope of such a repast. When this does not fill the available places, they are sent into the surrounding countryside to find more ('*make* them come in' means persuasion rather than coercion; Augustine was mistaken in using the word 'compel' to justify the use of force in dealing with unbelievers and heretics). Every seat must be taken, to prevent any of the original guests regretting their decision and hoping to be reconsidered; there will be no second chance.

There were two messages for those who heard the story the first time, one quite obvious and the other more subtle.

Clearly, it is a strong warning not to assume that one is sure of a place in the *future* kingdom, as Jesus' fellow-diner was probably doing. It is not those who believe in it, have received an invitation and are looking forward to it, who finally attend but those who make it top priority and come when called. Otherwise, they will see themselves replaced by the most unlikely substitutes.

But there is also an underlying claim that the kingdom is *present* as well as future. The first invitation came through the Hebrew prophets; the second has come through the person and work of Jesus himself. Everything is ready. The time for settling priorities is now. But the Pharisees are not 'coming' to the kingdom, though prostitutes and extortioners are eagerly seizing it. In passing, note that none of the excuses is an immoral or illegal activity; they are legitimate activities which, however, ought to be secondary but have become primary.

The second occasion (in Matthew) is in the temple courts of Jerusalem itself, during the last week of Jesus' life. The clash with the Jewish leaders is now public; the crisis is now reaching its climax. Not surprisingly, when Jesus tells the story for the second time, it is in much harsher terms, clarifying the underlying issues. The 'certain man' is now the king; the feast is a wedding reception for his son; the guests are given not one but two notifications of the time (does that refer to the re-telling of the story?); instead of simple evasion, the intended guests refuse and ignore the notice, abuse and murder the messengers; the host in anger kills them and burns their city (did Matthew record this after Jerusalem was razed in AD 70?); the vacant places are filled in a single rather than a double outreach. The stakes have been raised and the challenge is very much sharper.

But there is also an added twist to the story: a man arrives at the feast without changing his everyday clothing – and is thrown out. It was not an ancient custom to send suitable apparel with the invitation (that is a modern myth devised by expositors of 'imputed' righteousness!); but guests were expected to put on their best clothes. That this guest could have done so is clearly indicated by his 'speechless' reaction to the king's sympathetic enquiry ('Friend . . .', giving the man a chance to explain himself). Not to bother to get himself ready was as great an insult to the king and his son as declining to come at all.

The Pharisees who heard this extended version may have received this additional detail with some complacency. They would understand this reference to 'robes of righteousness', but they were already striving to attain such adornment. They would not realise (unless they had heard about his Sermon on the Mount) that Jesus considered their self-righteousness as totally inadequate to 'enter' the kingdom (Matt 5:20). The parable now contained a double warning against presumption – the kingdom is for those who come when called and who come properly prepared.

So much for the original (spoken) context. Now we must consider the later (written) one. Of the four gospels, two were compiled for the evangelism of unbelievers (Mark and Luke) and two for the encouragement of believers (Matthew and John; see John 20:31 for the latter's purpose, that readers may go on believing and may go on having eternal life).

Luke wrote for Gentiles (he was one and addressed one: Theophilus); Matthew wrote for Jews. The former used the term 'kingdom of God' without hesitation; the latter respected the Jewish reluctance to refer to the deity directly and usually used 'kingdom of heaven'. Luke applies the 'lost sheep' to sinners (Luke 15:4-7); Matthew applies it to backsliders (Matt 18:6,12-14).

Luke's readers would find the parable full of *comfort*. They would understand the invited guests who failed to turn up as the Jews who rejected Jesus, and the unexpected replacements as themselves, the Gentiles. The emphasis would be on the extended invitation to all and sundry. The parable has inherent 'gospel' appeal: 'Come, for everything is now ready . . . my house shall be full.'

Matthew's readers would find the parable full of *challenge*. They would understand those coming to the feast as themselves, the disciples who had 'come' to Jesus. While their first invitation was in no way related to their moral condition at that time (note 'both good and bad' in Matt 22:10), the feast itself certainly had moral implications and requirements. Invited guests needed 'robes of righteousness'.

Matthew is the gospel of 'righteousness'. It is the only gospel to point out that Jesus was baptised 'to fulfil all righteousness' (Matt 3:15, a sober reminder to those who do not see the necessity of baptism). Disciples are to make 'his kingdom and his righteousness' their over-all aim in life (Matt 6:33); only then can he be trusted to provide for all their other needs. Their righteousness must go well beyond that of the Pharisees (Matt 5:20).

This emphasis on righteousness (spelled out in considerable detail in the Sermon on the Mount) proves Matthew to be a 'Manual of Discipleship' for the early church, teaching new converts to obey everything Jesus commanded (Matt 28:20). Matthew understood perfectly well that we are not saved *by* righteousness, but we are saved *for* righteousness (cf Eph 2:8-10). In the parable, righteousness need not precede the invitation (which is to 'good and bad') but needs to precede the feast itself.

Theologians argue about 'imputed' and 'imparted' righteousness, one side claiming that the former is all that is required. Anxious to attribute every last morsel of salvation to the grace of God in Christ, they see *justification* (in which we are declared innocent by having our sins covered by 'his blood and righteousness') as the sole and sufficient qualification for entrance to the feast in the kingdom. But, laudable as the jealousy for grace may be, this view does not do full justice to the New Testament emphasis on the necessity of sanctification, if we are to see the king (Heb 12:14).

The parable itself implies this need for 'effort' on the part of the invited guests. Though the invitation is entirely gratuitous, those accepting it are responsible for changing their clothes. The whole of Matthew's gospel is a call for disciples to attain a practical righteousness of conduct and character. They are to hunger and thirst after it (Matt 5:6), so that what has been 'imputed' to them may also be 'imparted' to them, what has been credited to them in heaven may be cashed by them on earth.

This interpretation of the wedding clothes is in line with the rest of the New Testament. Luke, when recording words to disciples rather than sinners, stresses the need to be 'dressed ready' (Luke 12:35). Paul tells his converts to work out their salvation with fear and trembling, for it is God who works in them both to decide and to do the right things (Phil 2:13); he constantly uses the metaphor of changing clothes (cf 'put off' and 'put on' in Col 3:9-14). The book of Revelation does the same (Rev 3:4f,17f); the bride has 'made herself ready' by putting on the 'fine linen, bright and clean', which was 'given her to wear', the fine linen being a symbol of 'the righteous acts of the saints' (Rev 19:7f). Sanctification, like justification, is 'given' by grace; but also, like justification, it needs to be received, put on and worn.

Now we come to the crux of our study, and the reason for including it in a book on hell. What happens to the person who accepts the invitation and comes when called, but does not bother to change clothes? In theological terms, we are considering those who want justification, but not sanctification. In simpler terms, those who want to escape hell, but make no effort to get ready for heaven.

The answer is simple: they finish up in hell. Though the word itself is not used here, the appropriate language is: 'thrown outside . . . darkness . . . weeping and gnashing of teeth' (Matt 22:13). It is significant that these strong words are not applied to those who refused to come (though they were 'killed' and their city 'burned'), but to one who came but was not 'dressed ready'. The permanence of his fate is hinted at in the command to 'tie him hand and foot' (Matt 22:13) before being 'thrown' outside. He will neither be able to sneak back in nor snatch any food.

The words are not, of course, in Luke's version, since they belong to the extended part of the story in the second telling. Even had Luke known about it, he would probably not have used it. Writing for sinners, he must have noticed that Jesus rarely used such 'hellish' language with sinners (though sometimes with the self-righteous, but usually with his own disciples) and Luke followed his example. It is therefore to Matthew, collecting Jesus' sayings for his disciples, that we owe almost all our Lord's teaching on this awesome subject.

We have thus far ignored the statement with which the episode is concluded: 'For many are called, but few are chosen' (Matt 22:14). It is debatable whether this was Jesus' own conclusion or an isolated saying of Jesus which Matthew has appended (or even his own comment). Whichever, it is now part of the inspired Word of God and an integral element in this passage (note the: 'For . . . '). There are two main lines of interpretation.

One approach draws the main contrast between 'called' and 'chosen'. It usually considers the statement as an isolated entity, before relating it to the parable. Interpreted in a 'Calvinist' manner, the choosing takes place before the calling in time (in line with such texts as Rom 8:30: 'those whom he predestined he also called'). God may have commanded us to preach the gospel to the whole of mankind (Matt 28:19; Mark 16:15; Luke 24:47), but only the 'elect' will respond to the invitation and come to the feast. Since grace is irresistible, both for justification and sanctification, the elect will not only come but come appropriately dressed. Any who do not do so prove thereby that they were never 'chosen' anyway (it is usually said they were only 'nominal' or 'professing' believers who were never 'truly' born again).

There are some inconsistencies in this view. If 'chosen' here means 'elect, predestined', then what does 'called' mean? Calvinists believe in 'effectual' calling, which *always* succeeds in bringing those called, in effect making the 'called' and the 'chosen' exactly the same number! But in the parable the king 'called' those who refused to come (and did he not choose the original guest list?). The called are clearly a larger number than the chosen; and the king is the subject of both verbs. Does God, then, call many but only choose some, thus teasing the human race? Such an arbitrary deity is an offensive image impossible to reconcile with the God who 'so loved the world' (John 3:16) and 'desires all men to be saved' (1 Tim 2:4). The alternative is to give 'called' a human subject – human servants may call many (by public preaching), but their divine master will only choose few of the hearers. But if 'called' is thus released from its theological connotations, why retain them in 'chosen'? This seems an artificial division between the two verbs, apart from giving them two different subjects.

The other approach draws the main contrast between 'many' and 'few'. This time the statement is approached through the parable, rather than independently. Interpreted in an Arminian manner, the calling takes place before the choosing (in this context, but not necessarily elsewhere in the New Testament). This involves freeing both verbs from their theological content elsewhere in scripture. As a summary of the parable, the statement simply says that the number of those who are (finally) chosen is considerably less than the number of those who were (originally) called.

The many who were 'called' (the New International Version helpfully uses 'invited') included both those who didn't come and those who did. Both decisions were the full and free responsibility of the invitees and not the predetermined decree of the king. Likewise, the failure to prepare properly was the full and free responsibility of the person concerned and not the predetermined decree of the king. However, this in no way reduces the sovereignty of the king. He had the first choice in how many guests there should be and who should be invited. When they refused, he chose their replacements. And he had the final choice to reject the one not properly attired and retain those who were. But surely, someone will say, his will was frustrated by those who refused to come, thus limiting his sovereign choice. On the contrary, it was the king who chose not to force them to come; he could have sent soldiers to arrest them after he had sent servants to invite them. But he did not do so, preferring to have voluntary guests to honour his son. He chose rather to punish those who abused his messengers, thus displaying his sovereignty without dishonouring his son (by filling the celebration with sullen faces!). The king is in over-all control from beginning to end.

There remains one difficulty with this second view – the word 'few' does not quite fit the parable. There were almost as many final guests as were originally invited, and only one chair was vacant. Does the original number minus one deserve the title 'few'?

The discrepancy can be resolved if this statement is an addition to the parable by Matthew, either as a saying of Jesus from another context or as an inspired comment of his own (a practice much more common in John's gospel). With it, he is relating the essential thrust of the parable to the situation in the early church as he knew it. While in the story only one arriving guest failed to dress properly, Matthew was only too aware that a growing number of disciples in his day were falling into the same sloth and therefore facing the same danger of being rejected at the last. Indeed, a major motive in penning his gospel was to reverse the trend of 'many' hearing and accepting the good news but 'few' pressing on to clothe themselves in the righteousness of the kingdom.

His additional comment is all of a piece with the conclusion of the Sermon on the Mount (which was addressed to the 'disciples'; Matt 5:1), reminding them of the two 'ways' before them: the broad road to destruction, which many travel, and the narrow road that leads to life, which few travel (Matt 7:13f). The same thread runs right through the last of the five 'discourses' (or collections of Jesus' sayings) in Matthew; addressed to the Twelve, it warns of the eternal consequences of sloth in the servants of the Lord, describing these in the same terminology of hell as in this parable (Matt 24:45-25:46).

Who dare say that this message is irrelevant to the contemporary church scene? Cheap evangelism offers a guaranteed escape from hell on the slender basis of a repeated (one minute) 'sinner's prayer'. (For a considered appraisal of this doubtful procedure, see chapter 31 of my book *The Normal Christian Birth*, Hodder and Stoughton, 1989.) Deeds of repentance play little or no part (cf Luke 3:8; Acts 26:20). Holiness becomes an optional extra, entitling one to certain bonus blessings here and hereafter. This is not the gospel Matthew, or any of the apostles, preached.

After all, as servants of the King, our task is even more fundamental than persuading *guests* to attend the reception. We are actually helping the *bride* to ready herself for the wedding (John 3:29f; Rev 19:7f). For at the marriage of the Lamb, there will be no distinction between the two. It was for such a bride, holy and blameless, made up of guests who got themselves ready, that Jesus gave himself up on the cross (Eph 5:25f).

SCRIPTURE STUDY C:
THE DIVIDED FLOCK

Read Matt 25:31-46.

The parables of Jesus, apparently so simple when first read, become increasingly complex the more they are studied! Those who want to paddle in shallow interpretations soon find themselves out of their depth and must learn to swim or beat a hasty retreat. The parable of 'the sheep and the goats' is no exception.

But is it a 'parable' at all, or a straightforward prophecy about the future? And who are the 'brethren' of Jesus – Jews, Christians or the entire human race? Is this judgement individual or national in scope?

The passage is a favourite 'proof-text' for the importance of social action. Frequent quotation by preachers has helped foster the 'do-gooder' definition of a Christian. The decisive factor determining our eternal destiny appears to be our compassion for and care of those less fortunate than ourselves.

But isn't this salvation by works? The stress is on what we do for others, rather than what the Father or his Son do for us. There is no mention of the need for forgiveness of sin or holiness of character. Indeed, it would be difficult to see any relevance in the death and resurrection of Jesus, if this is the essential picture of the Day of Judgement. What happens to the gospel of grace?

Clearly, large issues are at stake here. The right questions must be asked and the right answers found. The Word of God must be thoroughly studied if it is to be handled aright.

PARABLE OR PROPHECY?

Perhaps readers have been misled by the fact that the preceding section of this 'Olivet' discourse comprises a series of parables relating to our Lord's return (the virgins and the talents).

These, while containing truth (or, rather, truths) are clearly fictional. The central character (who returns after 'a long time' away) is unnamed. The verbs are in the past tense, as if the events had already occurred.

All this changes with verse 31. The tenses are now future, the central figure is identified and the tenor is factual. The events have not happened yet, though they will.

Yet there is a parabolic element or, to be more accurate, the prediction includes an analogy ('*as* a shepherd . . . '). An observation from rural life (typical of the teaching of Jesus) is used to highlight a spiritual principle.

It is well known that Bedouin shepherds still graze sheep and goats together, though they are clearly distinguished by form and colour. Obviously, from time to time they have to be separated – for milking, shearing or sale. But it is also a daily occurrence, when the less hardy species is taken into the shelter of the fold for protection against the cold Middle Eastern nights. However, it is the observed fact of separation, rather than its purpose, which is the point of the analogy here.

Whether the shepherd always puts the sheep on his right hand is beyond this writer's knowledge. Verse 33 may be moving out of the metaphor and back into prophecy (or mixing metaphors, as with the shepherd who sets a table for the sheep in Ps 23:5!). If this verse is taken too literally, there will only be animals in heaven, or hell! We are back in the human scene, where the right hand is the position of honour and the left is the opposite.

It would also be a mistake to point out that sheep and goats are two different species, making their inherited nature the ground of their separation. This is often done in the interests of theology, interpreting the judgement as a simple division between the regenerate (sheep are born again) and the unregenerate (goats are born in sin), their distinct natures revealed in their different attitudes and actions. But this presses the analogy too far, turning it into an allegory. The simple simile (' . . . as a shepherd separates . . .') only emphasises what happens at the end of the day. In reality, as Jesus makes quite clear, the division is based on behaviour rather than breeding. We need to remember that he was addressing the twelve apostles, not the general public. Why did they need such a solemn warning?

We must not read any more into the analogy than Jesus originally intended. He was not claiming to be in the line of the shepherd-kings (though he actually was and is the Good Shepherd and the King of kings). He is here acting solely as the King on the throne of judgement, though he is judging those whom he has hitherto shepherded.

Nor is he emphasising the differentiation between the species. Some evangelical expositors have seized on this aspect to explain away the apparent implications for salvation by faith and the security of the believer. Though Jesus explains that they are separated on the ground of their behaviour, it is held that the real basis was their birth, what they were 'by nature'. In this view, the goats are the unregenerate (the old man in Adam) and the sheep are the regenerate (the new man in Christ), two quite distinct species, separated at the last by what they *are* rather than what they *do* – a view which renders most of the Judge's explanation of his verdict as irrelevant! In actual fact, the Son of Man will be dividing one (human) species, on the evidence of their actions (or lack of them).

When will this judgement take place?

WHICH JUDGEMENT?

Some readers may be surprised that this question needs to be asked. Surely this refers to the great Day of Judgement, before the 'great white throne', when the whole human race will be held accountable and the eternal destiny of every individual decided, following the return of Christ.

Would that it were that simple! However, one widespread opinion, known as 'dispensationalism' (associated with names like Darby, Scofield and Lindsay), has drawn a distinction between God's judgement of sinners (for punishment) and Christ's judgement of believers (for reward), as two entirely separate events. Matthew 25, which fits neither scenario, is yet a third judgement – of nations, as nations, for their attitude to the nation of Israel during the 'Great Tribulation' at the end of history (after the church has been 'raptured' out of the world).

Space forbids a thorough critique of this position (which interprets 'kingdom' in an exclusively future, Jewish and earthly manner). Suffice it to point out that God has appointed Jesus to judge the world (Acts 17:31), that visiting the sick and prisoners is hardly a national activity, that 'nations' refers to ethnic groups rather than political states, that 'separate one from another' indicates individual responsibility and that it would be unique for Jesus to call the Jews his 'brethren' (though Peter and Paul both did; Acts 3:17; Rom 9:3). Above all, the outcome of eternal life or punishment, destinies appropriate to individuals rather than nations, indicates that this is the final Day of Judgement.

However, there is also a problem for those who take a pre-millennial view of the future (note that while all dispensationalists are pre-millennial, not all pre-millennialists are dispensational). Taking Revelation 20 at face value, it appears that the resurrection of the righteous will take place at the Lord's return, which will be a thousand years before the general resurrection and the final judgement (see Scripture Study J for fuller details). So where does Matthew 25 fit in? Before or after this 'millennium' – since it appears to be the final judgement, yet takes place 'when the Son of Man comes'? The 'sheep' belong to the 'first' resurrection and the 'goats' to the 'second', yet both are here judged together!

It is a real puzzle, but might be resolved by recognising the biblical feature of prophetic foreshortening, the condensing of the future which brings together widely separated future events into one picture to highlight a moral choice in the present (one example is the Old Testament prediction of the Messiah's coming in 'the last days', which we now understand as two comings widely separated in time).

Of course, there is no problem for the post-millennial view (that the millennium will be the last thousand years of church history) or the a-millennial (that the millennium is the whole of church history, already nearly two thousand years). For both these the return of Christ is immediately followed by the Day of Judgement.

This discussion can, unfortunately, prove a real distraction from the fundamental message and challenge of this judgement, whenever it takes place. The important considerations are the *basis* of the judgement and its *results*.

BASIS OF JUDGEMENT

The people are separated on the ground of what they have *done*, not on the ground of what they *are*. It is their attitude, expressed in action, which is decisive. Scripture consistently teaches that all divine judgement is based on 'works', or deeds (cf Rom 2:6, quoting Ps 62:12 and Prov 24:12; 2 Cor 5:10; Rev 20:12).

But it is essential to notice that the criterion here is not just *what* has been done (or not done) but *who* it has been done to. The crucial point is, therefore, the identification of 'these brothers of mine'. To whom does Jesus refer?

The 'dispensational' view that this refers to the Jewish nation during the last days of world history seems altogether too *narrow*, both in time and space. There is no suggestion of such a limited application in the text itself. This interpretation seems to result from an attempt to fit the passage into a particular eschatological programme.

On the other hand, the usual 'liberal' view that this refers to any needy human being seems much too *broad* (and does much to encourage salvation by works). The universal brotherhood of man, and the universal fatherhood of God, are more characteristic of the 'social gospel' than the teaching of Jesus. He never included himself in the phrase 'our Father', referred to 'my Father' (as in verse 34) and only taught his disciples to call God 'Father'; indeed, it is doubtful if he ever used the word when speaking to the general public (pearls must not be given to pigs; Matt 7:6). In other words, Jesus only regarded those who had entered into a relationship with his Father through faith in himself as his 'brothers'. That is why he frequently used the term 'brethren' to describe his disciples (Matt 10:40,42; 12:48; 23:8; 28:10), but never used it of anyone else. It is the title most frequently given to his followers in the rest of the New Testament.

Before moving on, two minor points may be noted. In referring to '*these* my brethren', the 'king' would seem to indicate a group present on this occasion (it is easy to imagine him pointing at them). Is he directing attention to the sheep already on his right hand (is he telling the sheep to look around at their own group and the goats to look across at the other group)? Or is there a third unmentioned group between the sheep and the goats, either in front of or behind him? The former seems more likely. The other significant phrase is 'the *least* of these'. The least significant can be the most significant! Worldly assessments are totally inappropriate. The humblest of disciples is important to Jesus and of infinite value to him.

And he takes it *personally*. Whatever is done (or not done) for his disciples is done (or done) for him. This is not just because they are his 'relatives'. The solidarity is more than that of a family. As Israel was the 'apple of God's eye' (the iris, the most sensitive external part of the body), so Jesus' disciples are his body. To help or hurt them is to help or hurt him (as Saul of Tarsus discovered on the Damascus road, an eye-opener which blinded him! Acts 9:5).

This is the *real* basis of judgement. The separation is on the basis of each person's attitude to the 'king' *himself*, as evidenced (either positively proved or negatively denied) by their attitude to his followers. These are so bound up with him that it is sheer hypocrisy to profess to love him without loving them (1 John 4:20 points out that the brethren are the visible part of the Lord; if love cannot be demonstrated towards the visible, how can it be real towards the invisible?). Love of the brethren is an essential element of true discipleship (John 13:34) and the acid test of who is a child of God (1 John 3:10). It is highly significant that this description of the Last Judgement was not given to the general public but to the twelve apostles (Matt 24:3; note 'privately').

RESULT OF THE VERDICT

We can easily miss the essence of what follows by concentrating on the place rather than the person. It was not just *where* the two groups ended up but *who* they ended up with that is the more important feature.

Just as their attitude to the King has decided the issue of their destiny, so his presence or absence will be its main characteristic. The reward will be to *come* and share his kingdom (as his brothers they are also sons and heirs of his Father). To be with Father and Son is to be blessed, to enjoy the supreme quality of 'life', to inherit a legacy prepared from the beginning of time.

The punishment is to *depart* from him, to 'go away' from his presence for ever, which is to be 'cursed'. It is to share the same fate as the devil, in a situation that has also been 'prepared' beforehand.

In passing, we note that angels share both destinies. There are 'sheep' and 'goats' up there, as well as down here. There are angels loyal to the King, who already care for his brethren and who accompany him when he returns to earth. And there are others (one in three, if 'stars' in Rev 12:4 refers to them) who have joined the rebel archangel, Satan, and, as 'demons', oppress the King's brethren.

Both destinies are 'eternal'. At the very least, this means that the verdicts are final, without appeal or parole for the guilty and without change or cancellation for the acquitted. The use of the same adjective to qualify 'life' and 'punishment', when read in a simple and straightforward manner, seems to indicate that the one will last as long as the other (see chapter 3 for a discussion of whether 'eternal' means a quantity or quality of time; most scholars agree that it covers both). However, a growing minority claim that the *effect* of the punishment will be everlasting, but the *experience* of it will not. The guilty will be extinguished in the fire (which makes one wonder why the fire is 'everlasting'). This view distinguishes between punish*ment* (which is for all eternity) and punish*ing* (which is only for a time), the latter applied to conscious pain (which the Bible calls 'torment'). Yet the New Testament clearly states that the devil will be 'tormented day and night for ever and ever' (Rev 20:10). Presumably the same fate awaits those who join him in the fire. At any rate, the onus of proof is on those who claim otherwise. There is not a single hint in the passage itself that the fire will have one effect on the bad angels and an entirely different effect on bad humans.

THE ESSENTIAL MESSAGE

Sometimes we overlook the obvious by looking at the parts rather than the whole or by concentrating on thoughts rather than feelings. What is the most striking feature of this prophetic 'parable' of the sheep and the goats? Surely it is the element of surprise, which must have astonished the original listeners.

The Day of Judgement will be full of the unexpected. This is a constant theme on Jesus' lips. The first will be last and the last will be first. Not everyone who calls him 'Lord' or uses his name in 'deliverance' ministry will find themselves among the sheep (Matt 7:21-23).

Both the 'sheep' and the 'goats' express surprise, even shock, at the king's verdict. Both had been quite unaware of the significance of their activity (or inactivity). Perhaps the best things we do are those of which we are least conscious. The most offensive characteristic of self-righteousness is its self-awareness (Luke 18:11-12 is a classic case). The goats' reaction ('If we'd known it was *you*, we'd have done something about it') reveals that the fatal flaw in their attitude is still with them – they would still despise the 'least' and only help the important.

But the biggest surprise for today's reader comes from the context, and the fact that this was not addressed to the general public (who would probably have misunderstood it as much then as they do now) but to the *twelve disciples*. Yet the whole discourse (Matthew 24-25) is laced with warnings about hell! They themselves could finish up in outer darkness, weeping and gnashing their teeth, with the devil and his angels in the everlasting fire – as, indeed, one of their number (Judas Iscariot) actually did (John 6:70f; 17:12; Acts 1:25).

As if this were not enough, the emphasis throughout has been on sins of omission rather than sins of commission, things left undone rather than things done. Failure to feed the household, failure to get enough oil to keep the lamps burning, failure to use talents, failure to love the brethren – in a word, negligence! That alone earns 'a place with the hypocrites' (Matt 24:51).

The Twelve had begun by asking about the times and signs of Jesus' return to planet earth. He had satisfied their curiosity (except for the actual date, which even he did not know). Having done that, he turned their questions back on themselves (as he so often did), by telling them that his coming would precipitate a crisis for his own servants. Would they be ready?

The real test of their readiness would not be their reaction to the signs of his imminent appearing, but how they had behaved during the 'long time' he had been away (note the emphasis on delay in Matt 24:48; 25:5,19). Not what they were doing when he arrived, but what they had been doing (or, more particularly, *not* doing) while he had been away – this would be the real issue.

For all disciples, this passage provides powerful motivation – to be vigilant for his return, diligent in his service and benevolent towards his brethren. Sloth is, after all, one of the deadly sins, perhaps the deadliest and probably the most deadening.

SCRIPTURE STUDY D:
THE OPEN TOMBS

Read Matt 27:52-53.

When Jesus died, many strange things happened. The veil hiding the inner sanctuary of the temple was ripped apart (from top to bottom, indicating a divine rather than a human agent, for it was forty feet high). The sun was eclipsed for three hours (again, a supernatural rather than a natural event). There was an earthquake (which convinced the Roman officer in charge of the execution that Jesus was 'Son of God').

The earthquake had effects on the dead as well as the living, opening up many graves in the Kidron valley on the east side of Jerusalem. The landscape there is rocky, with little soil. Only the wealthy, like Joseph of Arimathea, could afford a hewn tomb; most were buried in very shallow graves, covered with stone slabs. These were shaken down the hillside by the tremor. The remains lay exposed to the elements. No one would think of repairing the damage over the Passover, since contact with the dead could mean ritual defilement. Had they done so, they would have been astonished to find that the bones had disappeared.

Three days later, during an after-shock, an angel rolled the stone away from Jesus' tomb. His body had also disappeared, leaving only the shroud. Later that same day, Jesus himself appeared to relatives, friends and disciples. Following that, the others who had left their tombs before him also appeared to those who had known them during their lifetime. What rumours must have swept the city that evening as shocked and stunned families sat pinching themselves to see if they had been dreaming!

So incredible is this part of the gospel story that to this day even

117

Christians seem embarrassed to mention it or even think about it. It's as if they have reached the limit of their credulity. Nevertheless, it is both possible and necessary to find meaning and significance in this extraordinary event.

But was it an event at all, or does it belong to that realm of legend which always surrounds the memory of unique historical personalities? For those who believe the Bible to be God's inspired Word (and words), the question does not arise – though even these seem to avoid this particular section of it. To others, one can only point out that Matthew was a tax-collector, an unlikely recipient of hallucinations or rumours! And it may be asked what possible reason he could have for passing on this information, other than that it happens to be true. He must have known it would reduce his credibility as a reliable witness.

The next comment to make is that once the resurrection of Jesus himself has been accepted, there is much less difficulty with that of others. Indeed, Jesus himself had raised others from the dead, usually only hours after their death (Jairus' daughter and the widow of Nain's son) but once after four days, when putrefaction had already set in (Lazarus of Bethany).

Other scriptures, too, contain similar happenings. On the Mount of Transfiguration (probably Hermon rather than Tabor) Jesus spoke with Moses and Elijah, who had both been dead for centuries. The witch of Endor enabled King Saul to encounter the dead prophet Samuel. It has to be added that in neither case is there any mention of empty tombs; they could therefore be classed as appearances of their spirits, rather than resurrection of their bodies.

There is a remarkable incident in connection with the prophet Elisha, in many ways a 'type' of Jesus (as Elijah was of John the Baptist). He had raised the dead (the son of a widow in Shunem, the next village to Nain) and fed a large crowd with a few small loaves. After Elisha was dead and buried, another funeral took place in the same cemetery; a band of raiders interrupted the ceremony and the man's body was hastily dumped in Elisha's tomb – whereupon the corpse immediately revived and stood to its feet!

So the incident in Matthew is only one of a series of such incidents, which all blur the boundary between the living and the dead. The one feature common to them all is the clear implication that death is not the end of an individual's existence, or even of bodily existence.

Accounts of emptied tombs are much more consistent with the Hebrew belief in the resurrection of the body than the Greek belief in the immortality of the soul. Hebrews also believed in an eternal Creator (who could make something out of nothing), whereas Greeks tended to believe in an eternal creation (Aristotle appears to be the first to teach a theory of evolution). Resurrection requires the supernatural intervention of a creative deity. To Matthew the resurrection of these 'holy' people would be proof enough of divine activity on that first Easter.

Nevertheless, questions remain. Who were the ones raised? Were Simeon and Anna among them? Did they speak to anyone or were they just seen? Where did they go to? Back to their tombs? To live on earth until they died again? Did they 'ascend to heaven' – before, with or after Jesus? Perhaps our curiosity will not be satisfied until we join them!

One aspect is genuinely perplexing, since it has doctrinal implications. What kind of bodies did they have when they appeared? Were their old bodies resuscitated (in which case they would have to die again, like Lazarus)? Or was it an appearance of their spirits (like Samuel, in which case their remains did not leave their opened tombs)? Or did they get glorious new bodies (like Jesus, in which case they would never die again)?

That third possibility raises huge problems. Not only would Jesus cease to be the 'firstborn' from the dead, in that they were raised three days before he was (though they were only seen afterwards); this would also be a unique exception to the principle that all the saints must wait for the resurrection of the body until Jesus returns to earth for his second visit (1 Thess 4:16). The Old Testament saints are included in this wait (Heb 11:40) and even the whole creation must be patient (Rom 8:22). The order of resurrection is clear: 'Christ, the *first* fruits; then, when he comes, those who belong to him' (1 Cor 15:23).

One thing can be said: the crucifixion of Jesus had cosmic repercussions. Not only did it cause an earthquake; it touched the world of the dead, releasing its inhabitants from their mortality. The gates of hades could not hold out against him who possessed the keys (Rev 1:18). The death of Christ was indeed 'the death of death'

119

(a phrase coined by the Puritan John Owen). For it was at his death, not his resurrection, that the tombs were opened and the dead released. The prince of this world, whose hold on the human race was the bondage of the fear of death (Heb 2:14f) was now himself driven out (John 12:31).

It is also significant that only 'holy' people were raised. This was not a redemptive but a rewarding act (and nothing to do with a later Christian tradition called 'The Harrowing of Hell'). In that sense, it was a foretaste of the 'first' resurrection of the righteous, rather than the second 'general' resurrection just before the Day of Judgement (Rev 20:5; see Scripture Study J).

However, it remains a unique event, testifying to the uniqueness of that other event of which it was the accompaniment. As such, it cannot be used to establish any Christian doctrine about the future; it stands on its own in the past. It says much for the authenticity of the gospel record that such an awkward piece of information was faithfully recorded. That encourages us to accept the account as it stands and humble ourselves before what we do not fully understand.

SCRIPTURE STUDY E:
THE RICH MAN

Read Luke 16:19-31.

Luke 16 contains two most unusual parables, one with ethical dilemmas and the other with theological difficulties! They could be entitled 'The good bad man' and 'The poor rich man'.

The second is our immediate concern, since it is the only parable to describe posthumous existence. It is also the only one to include proper names: Lazarus and Abraham (*dives* was attached later and is simply the Latin word for 'rich').

Four major questions of interpretation demand attention. First, is the imagery original to Jesus or traditional to Jews? Second, is the description factual (real people and places) or fictional? Third, was the reversed situation in the next world the result of material circumstances or moral character? Fourth, was the 'torment' in hades or in hell (i.e. before or after the Day of Judgement)?

Before tackling these, it will be necessary to look at both the context and the content of the story. Since the former usually indicates the thrust of the latter, it will be helpful to start there.

There are a number of links between what we call chapters 15 and 16 (remember that Luke did not divide up his narrative in this way, which often puts asunder what God has joined together); some of them are specifically verbal. The earlier chapter begins with *two* lost objects (a sheep lost far away and a coin lost at home; the former knew it was lost, the latter didn't) and continues with *two* lost sons (one far away, one at home), both with a commercial attitude to their 'prodigal' father, who not only gave them his money, but 'came out' to meet both of them.

It is significant that both stories in chapter 16 have an identical introduction: 'There was a rich man . . .'. The first of these corresponds to the younger son in the previous chapter – both 'waste' someone else's money (the verb is exactly the same in 15:13 and 16:1) and both eventually redeem the situation (one by returning home to meet his father and the other by cutting losses to make friends).

The second rich man corresponds to the elder brother. In both may be discerned the presence of selfishness and the absence of sympathy. It is important to note that the emphasis in both chapters is on *this* actor in the drama (though most evangelistic sermons highlight the younger son, for obvious reasons). Who does this second character represent?

It is significant that all but one of the parables in these two chapters are spoken to an audience of Pharisees (and their academic associates, the 'scribes'); indeed, the stories are pointedly directed at them. At the beginning, they are highly critical of Jesus' behaviour ('eating with sinners!'); later, they become cynical about Jesus' assertion that Mammon and God are incompatible objects of personal devotion. Since they managed to be both rich and religious, their arrogant self-righteousness could despise this penniless teacher.

Jesus charged them with contempt for the law (committing open adultery by divorce and remarriage) and contempt for the gospel (by not seizing it eagerly, as others were doing). Their claim to combine wealth with piety may impress their contemporaries but doesn't fool God, who knows the state of their hearts.

If the parable of the clever crook had shocked his hearers' morality, the next one would shake their materialism. With devastating clarity, Jesus contrasted the life of those who accumulate wealth in this world with their lot in the next. It is the strongest of his many warnings about the risks of riches.

The parable is constructed around a double comparison – between the two main characters and between the two phases of their existence (before and after death). The point is the total reversal of their circumstances. But the main focus is on the rich man (the beggar is silent throughout the saga); and he is deliberately left nameless, so that members of the audience could supply their own (in much the same way as Jesus had already challenged them to identify with the elder brother; cf 15:2 with 15:28-32).

The parable itself needs little comment. With great economy of words, Jesus painted a vivid, dramatic and memorable picture of the irrevocable fate awaiting those who have enjoyed the good life on earth. But it raises many issues of interpretation and application. We must now consider the four mentioned earlier.

ORIGINAL OR TRADITIONAL?

Was Jesus revealing new insights into the after-life or using old ideas? Was his basic understanding of the future fresh or familiar to his Jewish listeners?

There is, in the parable itself, the implicit claim that 'Moses and the Prophets' (what we call the Old Testament) contains sufficient warning about future punishment. Yet the fact remains that there is a paucity of such information in the Hebrew scriptures.

The most that can be said is that there is consistent teaching throughout about the righteousness of God and the inevitable judgement of sin. The day of reckoning is certain to come. There are also specific prophecies against building up wealth, especially if this includes exploitation of the poor, or indifference to their plight.

But the general assumption is that both rewards for good and punishment for evil will be given in this life. *Sheol* (the Hebrew equivalent of the Greek: *hades*), the world of the departed and disembodied spirits, is seen as a shadowy existence of unconscious inactivity – unable to communicate with each other or the Lord.

However, there is clear evidence that during the four hundred years between the Old and New Testaments, some Jews had developed much clearer concepts. While the liberal Sadducees retained their scepticism about survival beyond the grave (which is why they were sad, you see!), the more conservative Pharisees believed in resurrection, judgement, heaven and hell. Literature of the period (which we call the 'Apocrypha'; this means 'hidden', because they are not openly published in the 'canon', or 'rule', of scripture) contains a number of words and concepts found in Jesus' parable (e.g. in Enoch and 2 Esdras).

It looks as if Jesus' hearers would be quite familiar with his description of the after-life, especially since they were Pharisees (v.14).

Indeed, this is the parabolic method; like all good teaching, it begins with a situation or event which would be known to or understood by the audience (the only difference here is that the familiar was taken from the next life rather than this). The main purpose of the story was not to impart information but to challenge assumptions.

Every parable contains a surprise, an unexpected feature which is not familiar. In the present case, the shock is not *what* happened to the two men who died, but *which* it happened to! That the one suffering torment was one of God's chosen people (note 'Father Abraham' in v.24; cf John 8:39-41) and a rich one at that would have been a devastating blow to their complacency (then, as now, wealth was considered a sign of God's blessing and approval; poverty the opposite).

Our conclusion is that Jesus was working with their basic framework of thought about life after death, while introducing a startling twist to penetrate their comfortable arrogance. But was it the framework of his own thinking, as well as theirs?

FACT OR FICTION?

Is the parable 'only a story'? While accepting its challenge as real, do we take the rest of it as an accurate guide to the future? In using the thought-forms of his hearers, was Jesus stamping them with the approval of his own knowledge?

At one extreme, there are those who dismiss it as a myth containing a truth, a fable with a moral, to be treated as a product of imagination rather than a mine of information. The main point of the parable is the only part meant to be taken literally, or even seriously; the rest is fiction.

At the other extreme, there are those who do not regard this as a 'parable' at all. Starting from the unusual feature of a *named* character (the only instance in all the stories Jesus told), they see this as straight reporting of actual events which had already taken place – known to Jesus and possibly his audience as well. The exact number of surviving brothers (five) is another indication; the number is not essential to the narrative. They may even be among the listeners! The rich man is not named for reasons of delicacy. The great reversal of fortune is already past, not future (the verbs are all in the past tense – though this is a feature of all parables).

However, the story bears all the marks of a parable. The opening phrase is identical to the previous one ('There was a rich man . . .'). There is a good reason why one person had to be named, even though this does not identify the individual (see below). The style and structure are quite typical of the stories told by this greatest of all teachers.

But this does not necessarily mean that the fictional event could never happen in fact. Indeed, the 'reality' of the parables depends on the possibility that such things could and did happen (as is certainly the case with the previous four in these two chapters).

Would Jesus have chosen popular misconceptions to make his point? Would he give people a fright by describing a danger that would never materialise (scholars call such an 'existential warning')? Does this sound like the one who said: 'If it were not so, I would have told you . . .' (John 14:2)? Would one who always spoke the truth have used purely imaginary horrors to influence others?

If the picture does not correspond to reality, it is very misleading and could only give rise to groundless fears. Since this is one of the few occasions when Jesus spoke directly about the future of individuals, he must have realised that his words would be taken very seriously indeed and that they would be assumed to express his own convictions.

There is something in the parable itself which lends weight to the accuracy of his description. The climax and challenge is in the final part of the parable, namely, the failure of all six brothers to take seriously the words of warning already contained in their own scriptures. The Word of God is reduced to nonsense if 'this place of torment' is a figment of the imagination, either human or divine. It is inconceivable that Jesus would castigate such heedlessness with purely fictional threats. If Moses and the prophets are to be taken with deadly seriousness, how much more the warnings of the Son of Man who came down from heaven (John 3:12f).

In passing, we may note the relative evidential value of divine words and works, in Jesus' estimation. If the message is rejected, miracles are unlikely to convince. The demand for proof is spurious. Even a return from the dead would not remove scepticism. Imagine the reactions of the five brothers to the announcement: 'I've just returned from the dead and I've seen your brother in hell'! Actually, another 'Lazarus' did come back, as did the person who told this parable, but neither resurrection was sufficient to change the minds of those who would not believe (faith is still a matter of choice rather than evidence).

Accepting that Jesus was being honest about what could and would happen to his hearers, there are two more questions to face.

MONEY OR MORALITY?

Did the rich man suffer because he had been rich and was the poor man comforted because he had been poor? Is the next life simply a reversal of this one (as v.25 seems to imply), so that we can choose to live well here or hereafter, but not both? Is 'treasure in heaven' in direct ratio to poverty on earth? Is this why Jesus said: 'Blessed are you who are poor . . . but woe to you who are rich, for you have already received your comfort' (Luke 6:20,24)?

If it is as simple as this, then we shall have to preach a different gospel, one which excludes the need for atonement, for example. It will still be 'good news to the poor', in that they need to do nothing but remain poor to be sure of heaven! Isn't this precisely what Karl Marx called 'the opium of the people'?

Such may be the impression left by a superficial reading. But was the financial disparity the *only* difference between 'the tycoon and the tramp'?

Certainly, the rich man is not directly accused of private vice or public crimes. Nevertheless, he may be indicted of indulgence of self (note his dressing and eating habits, even his ornamental drive gates), indifference to others (he passed the beggar every time he went out) and ignorance of God (his Bible stayed on the shelf) – all fostered by his preoccupation with the good things of life. It is noteworthy that he sinned less in what he did than in what he left undone. We have already noted that sins of omission are just as likely to take someone to hell as sins of commission (see Scripture Study C).

Certainly, the poor man is not commended for any virtues either. But Jesus gave him a name and names in the Bible are significant, frequently pointing to the nature of a person. 'Lazarus' is the English equivalent of the Hebrew 'Eleazar', which may be freely translated: 'God-help-me' (what kind of circumstances was he born into that his mother would call him that?). Some have said this naming was a purely literary device to enable Abraham to refer to him, but it is surely more significant than that. Is not Jesus indicating that he looked to the Lord for support, when he received help from no one else? In other words, he was as dependent on the Lord as his counterpart was independent of him. Such is the typical effect of wealth, though not always the typical result of poverty.

Getting or having money is not in itself sinful – until it affects and takes over the one who has it. It is hard, but not impossible, for a rich man to enter the kingdom. Money can so easily take the place of God. It is impossible, not just hard, to serve God and Mammon at the same time (v.13).

God is the great revolutionary. He humbles the proud and exalts the humble. He fills the hungry with good things and sends the rich away empty (Luke 1:52f), though not necessarily in this world; most of the revolution will take place in the next. Then justice will be done and seen to be done.

But when will this be? When we die or after the Day of Judgement?

HADES OR HELL?

Does the suffering of those who are rich in material things but poor in spiritual things begin as soon as they die?

There are some surprising omissions from the parable; the picture is far from complete. There is no resurrection of the body or the Day of Judgement – and therefore no 'intermediate state' (see chapter 3). Above all, God is totally absent. The angels take one man to 'heaven' and Abraham tells the other to stay in 'hell'. There is no divine decision of declaration of the one's guilt or the other's innocence.

There is a further complication. When Jesus spoke of the place of punishment we call 'hell', he usually used the name 'Gehenna' (the garbage dump outside Jerusalem; see chapter 3). In this parable he uses 'hades', the name for the abode of disembodied spirits between death and resurrection.

The clear impression is that the rich man was in the 'flames of torment' immediately after his death, even while his brothers were attending his lavish funeral. So how does this fit in with the other revelations in the New Testament concerning our individual passage into the future?

One solution is to suppose that the sufferings of the lost begin before the Day of Judgement and are only made worse after that. Custody before trial is already a painful experience, rather than a neutral wait. Some annihilationists teach conscious suffering up to the Day of Judgement and oblivion thereafter (this unusual reversal of judgement and punishment has the perverse effect of making the Day of Judgement something sinners can look forward to!).

However, there are cogent reasons for believing that Jesus is referring to the ultimate rather than the immediate state after death. The language ('dip the tip of his finger in water and cool my tongue') implies a bodily existence. Fire is always associated with hell, as is intense thirst. 'Torment' and 'agony' hardly imply that the suffering is mild.

We believe that the true explanation is that for the purpose of this parable, the picture has been deliberately simplified. All incidental information has been left out, irrelevant events excluded. Time has been condensed: the three phases of our existence have been telescoped into two (such 'prophetic foreshortening' is a common feature in scripture). 'Hades' is not here a specific title for the intermediate state, but a general term for posthumous existence.

It needs to be remembered that Jesus was not answering an enquiry about the future, but challenging an attitude in the present. The parable was an attack on those who were sneering at his warnings about wealth. The weapon of his tongue (which resembles the slashing two-edged sword of the Roman soldier) was sharpened by honing the story down to its bare essentials.

Everything he said was true to reality, but it was not the whole truth about reality – and was never meant to be. To have included the whole future programme would have made the parable as long as the book of Revelation, and buried the real point in a mass of detail. It remains to draw out the truths that are emphasised in the parable.

Death is not the end of conscious existence. The essential personality survives, with memory intact. Communication with others is characteristic of life both before and after death.

For some, life beyond will be far better than life here, while for others it will be far worse. The difference is the direct result of the character of life here. Many are in for a big surprise.

Destinies are fixed at death. The future is then irrevocable because the past is unalterable. There are only two possibilities, with a 'fixed gulf' between them. Nor is it possible for the dead to influence the living (or, conversely, for the living to help the dead).

Hell is horrible. In this parable, the flames torment, but do not annihilate. The agony is physical as well as mental. There is an awareness of being excluded from 'heaven', cut off from the people of God.

All of these facts are confirmed elsewhere in the teaching of Jesus, much of which is not in the immediate context of this parable. Put negatively, nothing said here is inconsistent with any of his direct statements about the future.

If we do not take Jesus' words as seriously as he intended, we would not be convinced of their accuracy even if the rich man himself came back to warn us. The sceptic will continue to live as if he is not rich (unlike some others) and as if he is not going to die (unlike all others). This parable shatters such self-deception.

SCRIPTURE STUDY F:
THE DYING THIEF

Read Luke 23:39-43.

If the parable of the rich man in Luke 16 emphasises that death terminates the opportunity of getting right with God, the incident of the dying thief in Luke 23 emphasises that the door is open right up to the moment of dying. Only eternity will reveal how many 'death-bed' conversions have been inspired by this incident.

However, unlike many of them, the plea in this case was quite spontaneous. No one, not even Jesus, was urging him to make his peace with God before it was too late. If anything prompted the dying man to say what he did, it was his fellow-criminal's sarcastic insulting of Jesus ('You're supposed to be the Messiah – then do your stuff and get us out of this'). Even this impudent challenge contained a grudging admission that he had helped many others out of their troubles (a fact widely known and accepted).

The bearing of Jesus throughout the degrading procession and agonising crucifixion (from which comes the word 'excruciating') must also have made a profound impression, particularly when he begged forgiveness for those responsible – the very opposite of the usual reaction of victims, which was to curse and blaspheme.

Nor must we overlook that he was Jewish and had a religious background, though a bad moral record. He was convinced that God would send an 'anointed king' (in Hebrew: *meschiah*; in Greek: *christos*), who would inherit a throne and establish a kingdom. No doubt the notice pinned to the cross above Jesus' head also made a contribution to his train of thought (whereas his own 'accusation' read 'Robber', Pilate, more as an act of impotent defiance than of moral courage, had written for Jesus: 'King of the Jews').

His request reveals profound insights into the realities of the situation. His honest assessment of himself reveals real *repentance*. Recognising and accepting that his punishment at man's hands is justly deserved, he has retained the greater fear of meriting penalty from God's hands. He is amazed that his partner is willing to risk that as well. This fear of God is an essential element in true penitence and is the beginning of wisdom. His own guilt is magnified by the innocence of the 'man' on the next cross, whom he now addresses for the first time – by name (has he just heard it, or has he known it for some time?).

His request reveals remarkable *faith*. Not only does he believe that Jesus is 'King of the Jews' (probably the only one who did at that moment); he is also convinced that this dying man will one day receive his kingdom. That he thinks this will only happen in the distant future is implied by his asking to be 'remembered'; it will be far enough off for him to have been forgotten. This also means that he believed in a future resurrection (both for Jesus and himself) when that time came. These underlying assumptions have a strong Messianic flavour, nearer to the creed of the Pharisees than the Sadducees.

Jesus' reply also reflects contemporary Jewish thinking. 'Paradise' was originally a Persian word meaning 'walled garden' and was particularly used of palace grounds (since few other than kings had such places), where the king would stroll with his favoured friends. The word conveyed the feeling of being greatly honoured (as would an invitation to a Buckingham Palace garden party). By the time Jesus used it, the Jews were probably already applying it to a special section of 'hades', reserved for those who were particularly righteous in God's sight and worthy of his nearer presence (roughly equivalent to 'Abraham's bosom' in Luke 16:22). Clearly, Jesus did not need to explain the term; the dying thief understood it perfectly well.

The most significant word, however, is 'Today'. There will be no need for Jesus to search his memory to recall the thief, because their relationship, established in such unusual circumstances, would not be interrupted but enhanced by their imminent death. They would be together later that same day – free from their painful and humiliating situation.

Jesus' promise surely implies that they would both be fully

conscious and able to communicate with each other. What real comfort could there possibly be in a shared coma? Still some persist in asserting 'soul-sleep' between death and resurrection; often rearranging this text: 'Today I say to you: we shall be together in Paradise'. Paul was hardly likely to 'desire to depart and be with Christ, which is better by far' (Phil 1:23), if it meant ceasing to be conscious of their relationship. The phrase 'fallen asleep' is simply a euphemism for the moment of death, based on the appearance of the body when the spirit has departed from it.

There is an even deeper significance in the word 'Today'. Since Jesus' advent, the coming kingdom is present as well as future, both now and not yet. It can be entered and enjoyed already, though it will not be established and cannot be inherited until later. The future has invaded the present. Tomorrow is now part of today. 'If I drive out demons by the Spirit of God, then the kingdom of God has come upon you' (Matt 12:28). The technical term used by theologians to describe this dimension of the kingdom that is now 'at hand' (i.e. within our grasp) is 'realised eschatology'.

This is an essential element in the gospel. There are many examples of this 'time-warp', but one sums them up: the raising of Lazarus (John 11:1–44). After Lazarus' death, Jesus comforted his sister Martha by telling her that her brother will rise again, but she found little consolation in the thought, since she saw it as a distant event, far into the future ('at the last day' of history). Jesus then assured her that since he himself *was* the resurrection and the life, the future could be transferred to the present for those who believed in him. In response, Martha became the first woman to verbalise the belief that Jesus was 'the Christ, the Son of God, who was to come into the world' (v.27; some weeks before, Peter had been the first man to make such a confession). In spite of pragmatic scepticism ('by this time there is a bad odour, for he has been there four days'), her faith in Jesus was rewarded by witnessing first-hand at one tomb what will one day happen at every resting-place of the dead (John 5:28f). Lazarus' spirit was reunited with his body (though it must be pointed out that it was his rejuvenated old body, which later had to die again – unlike the unique resurrection of Jesus, which more truly prefigured the 'last day').

The brief encounter between the dying Saviour and the dying

thief is rightly considered one of the most inspiring incidents in the gospel account. But too much can be made of it. Luke never intended it to be used as a norm for Christian conversion, nor a precedent for the minimum qualifications required to escape hell and enter heaven. (I have looked at the serious implications of this misapplication in chapter 9 of *The Normal Christian Birth*, Hodder and Stoughton, 1989).

The poor man was not in a position to be baptised in water or Spirit (he was in the wrong place for the one and the wrong time for the other!). He could neither express his gratitude nor earn a reward through faithful service. He never heard the full gospel (which includes the events of Easter and Pentecost).

What he did have was a personal relationship with the Lord Jesus which would be unaffected by death – and that is the heart, if it is not the whole, of our hope for the future.

SCRIPTURE STUDY G:
THE TESTING FIRE

Read 1 Cor 3:10-15 and 5:1-12.

It is commonly assumed that Christians will never be judged. Chapter 8 of Paul's letter to the Romans is the favourite 'proof-text' for this assumption: it begins with 'no condemnation' and ends with 'no separation'.

Many fail to notice the present tense in the statement 'There is *now* no condemnation for those who *are* in Christ Jesus' (Rom 8:1; note 'now are' is not 'once were'). This can only be said of those who continue to 'abide' in Christ; branches that do not remain in the vine are cut out and burned (John 15:6).

There is also a significant omission in the list of persons and things unable 'to separate us from the love of God that is in Christ Jesus our Lord' (Rom 8:39), namely, ourselves. Just a little further on in the same letter, Paul reminds the 'saints' at Rome that their position in God's purposes is conditional, 'provided that you continue in his kindness, otherwise you also [as well as 'some' of the Jewish branches] will be cut off' (Rom 11:22).

Throughout the New Testament epistles (all of which are addressed to believers and not unbelievers) are scattered a number of clear statements that the readers will be judged. Readers may care to look up Romans 2:1-6, asking who Paul is addressing as 'you' (in the light of Rom 1:7) and who he refers to as 'we' in Romans 14:10. In his correspondence with the Corinthians he is unequivocal: 'For we must all appear before the judgement seat of Christ, that each one may receive what is due him for the things done while in the body, whether good or bad' (2 Cor 5:10).

Some attempt to tone this down underlies the claim that this judgement is 'only for the purpose of assessing rewards for faithfulness'. But surely punishment is due for the 'bad' things done in the body, not just loss of reward.

Others cling to the hope that one of the texts we are now considering (1 Cor 3:10-15) reveals the very worst that could happen to believers in such judgement. That is, the believers themselves would still be saved, but would suffer considerable loss of approved record and appropriate reward.

Some even suggest that this 'trial by fire' is all that Jesus was referring to when he warned his own disciples about hell. In other words, 'hell' for them would mean the loss of everything but their salvation. The 'weeping and gnashing of teeth' would be for what they had lost, not because they themselves would be lost.

Will the text bear this interpretation? Is this indeed the very worst that could happen to a believer? Is the Christian absolutely certain to finish up in heaven, even though he has lost everything he hoped to bring with him? The passage must be carefully unpacked.

First, let us clear out of the way any supposed connection between this passage and the subject of hell. Paul is not here referring to the final punishment, but the final judgement. There is no trace of any suggestion that someone could pass through the 'lake of fire' and emerge singed, but saved. Hell is not purgatory. Those consigned there, remain there.

The fire referred to here is the fire of judgement rather than the fire of punishment. It is the fire of God (cf Heb 12:29) rather than the fire of hell. It is the fire that refines metal and burns up dross, making good things better and bad things worse.

Second, the fire is not applied to the people themselves, but to their deeds. It is their work that is being 'fired', their achievements rather than themselves.

In particular, it is their service for Christ and his church that is being examined. Activity which they themselves and others would consider to have been good and even godly must now be tested to see if it has any lasting value in God's purposes.

It is, alas, possible to be very busy in the work of the church, yet to be doing it in the wrong way, at the wrong time, from the wrong motive, for the wrong purpose and with the wrong people.

It is not the quantity, but the quality, of our service that matters in the long run.

Paul is particularly concerned about the workers who have followed his pioneering ministry. He has planted communities of the kingdom in virgin territory (Rom 15:20). But apostles must keep moving on to fresh fields, leaving their infant fellowships for others to nurture.

It was vital that his successors continue to follow his own principles, or the churches would be broken down rather than built up. As an 'expert builder' (Paul did not suffer from that false modesty which counterfeits true humility), he had made sure his converts were rooted and grounded in Christ, and no one else. This was the solid 'foundation' of his church-planting work. What was built on that by other ministries could vary enormously.

From the context, we learn about that form of 'jerry-building' which gave Paul the greatest concern. Work that focuses attention on a human personality, that makes too much of one ministry, that causes believers to become followers of a man, that glorifies a human name, that makes disciples of one of Christ's servants rather than Christ himself – all this takes the pre-eminence away from the Lord who should have it undivided. He is not only the sure foundation; he must be the whole building.

Perhaps this is why there is no trace of one-man ministry in the New Testament. Apostles always travelled in pairs, often with larger teams. Local elders were always plural. There is safety in numbers. The Lord never gives all the necessary gifts to one of his servants, even though he had them all himself.

It is man-centred ministry that will not stand the test of fire. However, most ministries are a mixture of temporal and eternal elements. Therefore, there is a much greater number and variety of results from this testing (it is not called a 'judgement'). This is expressed in the list of material metaphors – from the most precious (gold) and still valuable (silver), both of which are purified by fire, through that which remains unaffected (costly stones), that which takes time to be combusted (wood) and, finally, to that which quickly disappears in the flames (hay or straw). Unlike this test, all events labelled as 'judgements' in the New Testament reveal only two categories.

How much this reminder is needed in this day of 'successful' churches and ever-increasing number of para-church organisations, so often built around one man's vision or gift. Divine criteria for evaluating ministry may be very different to ours.

Third, and this point is crucial, this passage is concerned with serving rather than sinning. It is about ministerial achievement rather than moral abuse, the testing of activities that are intentionally good rather than deliberately bad. Paul is not here dealing with backsliding, much less apostasy.

This is the worst that can happen to a Christian worker whose service for the Lord is just not good enough, but who is at least trying to do something worthwhile, even if he fails.

But it is not the worst that can happen to a Christian who wilfully continues in the sins of his former life or indulges the flesh in quite new ways. Later in this same letter, Paul reveals, almost inadvertently, what he believes can happen to these. He lists some of their past transgressions – 'adulterers, male prostitutes, homosexual offenders, thieves, greedy, slanderers, swindlers' – and makes it absolutely clear that such will 'never inherit the kingdom of God' (1 Cor 6:9f). That he applies 'never' to believers as well as unbelievers is shown in his parallel statement to the Galatian brothers. After a similar list of such 'works of the flesh' he says: 'I warn you, as I did before, that those who live (literally, 'go on living' – the tense is present continuous) like this will not inherit the kingdom of God' (Gal 5:21).

This danger is also mentioned in the second passage we are looking at in this epistle (1 Cor 5:1-12). One of the members of the Corinthian church was openly living in an incestuous relationship with his own mother (or step-mother; 'his father's wife' could mean either). So even the early church had its scandals, which those who idealise that first period need to remember.

The situation must be corrected immediately. The obvious reason for this is the reputation of the fellowship and the credibility of the gospel. But Paul is also concerned about the risk to the man involved. Since he does not appear to have responded to rebuke, the members as a whole (and not just the elders) must exercise discipline. They must abandon their indifference to the situation, and their arrogance (what were they proud about – their broad-mindedness?) and take two further steps in dealing with the miscreant.

The first is excommunication: the miscreant must be put out of fellowship. This would involve refusal to eat with him, not just at the Lord's table but other meals as well. There comes a point where it is impossible to disassociate from the sin without disassociating from the sinner who refuses to renounce his sin. Note that this only applies to sinners inside and not outside God's people.

The second is more drastic and is the final sanction any church can impose on one of its members. In a solemn and shared act, the fellowship must hand over its member to Satan (whether he is directly addressed, as well as the person concerned, we are not told). The purpose of this is clear – that the devil, source of all disease and death, may so affect his body that its carnal lusts may no longer be exercised (Paul's use of the word 'flesh' is a little ambiguous; he uses it both in a neutral way for the body and in a negative way for the fallen nature, the latter using the former as its instrument).

It cannot be too strongly emphasised that the purpose of this radical ritual is redemptive. In thus bringing the sin to an end, by inviting Satan to 'destroy' the flesh, his spirit will be saved on the day of the Lord (i.e. the Day of Judgement). He may lose his body, but he will keep his soul.

The implication is obvious, but rarely deduced. If the man is allowed to continue in sin and the church does nothing about it, he could well reach the point of no return and his spirit would *not* be saved on that day. The church would lose one of its members – for ever. If he goes on sowing to the flesh as he is doing, he will reap a harvest of destruction (Gal 6:7f; another warning addressed to believers). At the moment of writing, Paul gauges that he has not yet gone too far and can still be 'saved', but only if the church acts quickly on his behalf. Otherwise, he will slip 'beyond redemption'.

A similar exhortation appears in the letter of another apostle (1 John 5:16f). Here the remedy for a brother who is observed committing a sin (note that this is a single act, not a continual habit) is loving intercession. Yet here too, there can come a point where the sin is too serious for prayer to be of any use. 'There is a sin that leads to death' (John does not specify what it is). There is a possibility of backsliding beyond the reach of praying brothers (and the listening Father).

Yet another New Testament writer, the anonymous author of the epistle to the Hebrews, makes the same point. His warnings cover simple neglect (Heb 2:1–3), public apostasy (Heb 6:1–8) and deliberate persistence in sin (Heb 10:26f). He seems to take it for granted that salvation can be lost, but goes much further in asserting that, once lost, it can never be regained (Heb 6:6), though he reassures his readers that he is confident that this will not happen 'in *your* case' (Heb 6:9), which does not mean that he doesn't believe it could happen in *any* case. These statements and, indeed, the thrust of the whole letter are often described as 'difficult', but are only so to those who come with minds already committed to the dictum: 'once saved, always saved'.

To sum up our thoughts on these two passages in the Corinthian correspondence, there is a fundamental difference between serving and sinning, when we stand before the judgement seat. The compromised servant will be separated from his service and will not be condemned with it. The continual sinner will not be separated from his sinning and will be condemned with it. To the Lord, holiness is of much greater importance than busyness.

SCRIPTURE STUDY H:
THE SECOND CHANCE

Read 1 Pet 3:17–4:6.

We have no record of Peter's encounter with the risen Jesus on that first Easter Sunday (1 Cor 15:5) and therefore no idea what each said to the other on that occasion. However, it is at least possible that Peter, with his usual impetuous curiosity, asked Jesus where he had been and what he had been doing during the missing seventy-two hours (most of the evidence suggests that Jesus died at 3 p.m. on Wednesday, 14th of Nisan, AD29 and rose between 6 p.m. and midnight on the following Saturday, the 'first day' of the Hebrew week beginning at sunset; this would allow for his predicted 'three days and nights' in the tomb by Hebrew reckoning and his rising on 'the third day' by Roman reckoning; the Sabbath following his death was not Saturday, but the special Sabbath of the Passover – John 19:31).

Jesus' reply, as to his whereabouts and activity between his death and resurrection, may be found in a letter which Peter wrote many years later, containing an extraordinary piece of information. This is rarely shared in the pulpit, not least because most Holy Week services terminate on Good Friday, only being resumed on Easter Sunday morning – leaving the congregations to assume Jesus did nothing of any significance during the interval!

Taking the passage in its 'plainest and simplest' sense, it appears that Jesus went and preached the gospel to those who were already dead (and therefore in 'hades')! But not to all of them; his congregation was composed of that whole generation which was drowned in the flood at the time of Noah.

Such is the astonishing account which Peter, and Peter alone, gives of those hidden days. Yet he mentions it almost incidentally, with no sense that his readers will find it sensational or incredible. Indeed, he introduces it as accepted, or at least acceptable, fact, proceeding immediately to its practical application. He uses it to stimulate godly living and uncomplaining suffering.

Peter would have been astonished to know how much speculation and controversy has been aroused by his revelation, unfortunately focusing on what he said, rather than why he said it. These verses have been described as 'one of the most difficult passages in the New Testament'. This kind of comment always prompts the question: difficult to understand or difficult to accept?

There have been many and varied attempts to 'explain' what Peter meant, most of which seem to explain it away! We list a few of them below.

Some change the *audience*. Jesus is said to have preached to all the 'righteous' souls from all previous centuries, so that he could transfer them from 'hades' to 'paradise'. Jesus is said to have preached to the fallen angels, the 'gospel' being the bad news of their defeat and doom. Jesus is said to have preached to all those who had 'never heard', which means all the Gentiles and possibly some Jews.

Some change the *timing*. They make it much earlier – the pre-existent Son of God was himself preaching just before the Flood, in spirit rather than in body, of course. Or they make it a little later – Jesus was preaching after his resurrection, in a 'spiritual' body, of course.

Some change the *text*. Arguing that a copyist's mistake has crept into the manuscripts, they 'emend' the Greek to read that it was Enoch, Noah's great grandfather, not Jesus, who preached to the generation that would perish in the flood. This alteration creates another problem: the reference no longer makes any sense in Peter's context.

It is hard to avoid the impression that most, if not all, such suggested 'explanations' are really motivated by an extreme reluctance to accept Peter's account as it stands, since they appear to be attempts to 'get round' what he is claiming to have happened. Can we identify a possible reason for this hesitation? There is one very obvious possibility.

The general teaching of the Bible is that the opportunity of reconciliation between sinful humans and a holy God is strictly limited to this life. Death ends this possibility and seals eternal destiny. This gives an urgency to both the preaching of the gospel and the need to respond to it.

Yet Peter seems to be contradicting this basic assumption, by apparently teaching that the gospel can continue to be communicated after death, the implication being that it can also continue its redemptive work when accepted by the dead. If this is true, the urgency of seeking salvation is jeopardised; indeed, sinners would be encouraged to procrastinate ('there's always plenty of time to think about that, whether this side of the grave or the other'). Further, by thus prolonging the opportunity of salvation, the door is opened to 'universalism' (see chapter 2), the hope that, sooner or later, everybody will be saved.

The fear that the incident will be 'used' in this way is very real, though nothing could be further from Peter's own application of it. That the anxiety is not unfounded may be seen in the comment on this passage by one of the twentieth century's most influential biblical scholars, William Barclay, who says it contains 'a breath-taking glimpse of nothing less than the gospel of a second chance'.

However, fear of heresy is not always helpful to sound exegesis, tending to antithesis rather than synthesis. Fear of relativism can lead to an unscriptural absolutism. To allow any exception to a rule can seem to undermine and ultimately abolish the rule. The exception becomes a 'loophole' which is gradually stretched to the point where the rule becomes the exception! That this can happen is easily illustrated.

Divorce is a case in point. Jesus' rule on this was clear: all remarriage is adultery in God's sight (Mark 10:11f; Luke 16:18). Yet he made *one*, and only one, exception: where the divorce was on the ground of adultery (Matt 5:32; 19:9). Some Christians fear that allowing *any* exception would fail to arrest the trend towards general acceptance of all divorces and remarriages, even in church circles – and there is considerable justification for this forecast. Yet in denying any exception, they have become more rigid than the Lord himself.

The case we are considering is very similar. The rule of scripture is clear. Death does fix a 'great gulf' which cannot be crossed (Luke

16:26; see Scripture Study E). To seek God and find him is the primary purpose of life (Acts 17:27). The opportunity to do so will last as long as life itself; the door is open until the moment of death, as the dying thief discovered (Luke 23:40–43; see Scripture Study F). But then it is closed for ever.

However, there is this one exception. It does not apply to all the dead, or even to most of the dead. Specifically, it only applied to one generation of human beings, from the time of Noah. They are the only exception there has been, nor is there any hint elsewhere in scripture that there will ever be another. It is therefore possible to accept this one exception without endangering the general rule. There is certainly no basis here for 'universalism', or even what Tennyson called 'the larger hope' of a second chance. It is an abuse of scripture to make an exception into the rule.

Human curiosity naturally wants to know why there was this single exception. We are not told. Any 'explanation' is pure speculation. Yet there is one possible reason, entirely consistent with the justice of God. Why should one generation have the privilege of a second chance, unless they had not had the normal first chance? God had singled them out as an example of his ability to destroy an evil world; but had then promised that he would never do that again to any succeeding generation, until the very end of history. This could be used to accuse him of injustice, treating that generation quite unfairly – a charge which a righteous God would never allow to be made against himself. So, to that generation which had suffered a unique experience of his judgement, he gave a unique opportunity of his grace and mercy (1 Pet 4:6 clearly implies they were being offered salvation).

Of course, this is all pure guess-work. God is not accountable to us and does not need to justify his actions by disclosing his reasons. There is a place for reverent agnosticism. If we knew all the answers, we would be God. He has told us what he wants to tell us and what we need to know. The very unlikely and unexpected nature of this revelation is witness to its truth.

In passing, it may be noted that, if the incident really happened, there can be no doubt that the disembodied spirits of those who have died are fully conscious and able to communicate with each other. I wonder if Noah and his family were present on that unique occasion and, if so, what their feelings were. I must remember to ask them!

But it is far too easy to be carried away by such thoughts or to get caught up in the sensational aspects of the incident. The result is that Peter's very practical purpose for introducing it is completely overlooked. His intention was to encourage ethical application rather than intellectual speculation. Not that his train of thought is all that easy to follow (Paul could have returned Peter's complaint that 'his letters contain some things that are hard to understand'; 2 Pet 3:16)!

We can begin by identifying two threads which run right through this letter to young Christians scattered throughout what we now call Turkey.

One is their need to *accept suffering*. Nero was now the Roman emperor and ripples of his hostility towards disciples of Jesus were spreading through the empire. It has always been part of discipleship training that 'we must go through many hardships to enter the kingdom of God' (Acts 14:22). The need for such encouragement was becoming more acute. But, like Christ before them, they must suffer for doing right, not wrong.

The other is their need to *avoid sinning*. It is precisely their moral difference from their neighbours that aggravates the persecution, which brings the pressure to revert to the pagan immorality which had been their former way of life.

The two needs are interrelated and Peter reinforces his exhortation by distinguishing between 'body' and 'spirit' (the two key words in this passage; trace them through). It is not what is done with or to the body that is most important but what is done with and to the spirit. A preoccupation with the body, whether protecting or indulging it, can lead to the neglect of the spirit. The body may be destroyed, but the spirit survives. This is precisely what happened to Jesus, who was put to death in the body but made alive in the spirit, to continue his gospel ministry elsewhere.

Baptism, the believers' passage through water, 'saves' them from their sinful generation, just as Noah and his family were saved from theirs by the flood (cf Acts 2:38-40, part of Peter's first sermon). But baptism does not save by washing the body but by cleansing the spirit (appealing to God for a good conscience). The new life, to which they have been raised and in which they now walk (cf

Rom 6:4), inevitably brings with it the suffering of the righteous, which proves that they are 'done with sin' (4:1), finished with the wrong desires of the flesh.

When believers are more concerned about their spirits in the future than their bodies in the present, they will be more influenced by the will of God than the ways of men. They will rejoice when they are persecuted for righteousness, for great is their reward in heaven (Matt 5:11f).

From the lips and life of his Lord, Peter had learned his lessons well. Like his Lord, he would finish up being put to death in the body on a cross (but upside down at his own request, feeling unworthy to be in the same position). And he would endure it, despising the shame, for the joy set before him, knowing that he too would be made alive in the spirit and with his Lord for ever.

SCRIPTURE STUDY I:
THE FALLEN ANGELS

Read 2 Pet 2:4-10 and Jude 6.

The Bible takes it for granted that human beings are not at the top of the scale of God's creatures. Though above the animals, they are 'a little lower than the angels' (Ps 8:5). This presents a problem to the evolutionist, though not to the creationist!

Angels are superior to us in strength, intelligence, motion and adaptability. Originally inhabiting heavenly places, they can freely visit earth and, as we shall see, be thrown into hell. Though they had a beginning, they have no end, for they are inherently immortal, unlike man. They have been 'born', but they cannot die. Their number, though huge, is fixed. They neither reproduce nor increase. This does not make them immortal in the divine sense; God alone has the immortality that has neither beginning nor end.

They can sin, but they cannot be saved. Jesus did not and would not shed his blood for them. That is not because they are incapable of receiving forgiveness, but because grace has not been extended to them – possibly because they had already known the glorious life of heaven and yet rejected it. The leader of their rebellion against God's rule is known by various names (Lucifer, Satan and Beelzebub), described by various metaphors (the dragon, the ancient serpent, the prowling lion) or is simply referred to as the 'devil'. One third of the heavenly host defected with him (Rev 12:4) and are now known as 'demons', 'evil' or 'unclean' spirits. Those who remained faithful to their Creator are sometimes called 'deities' but, more frequently, 'sons of God'.

It is with a small section of this rebel group that we are presently concerned. Their sordid story begins in the days preceding the Flood (and may be found in Gen 6:1–6). From this it appears that angelic beings could experience sexual attraction for human females and were capable of seducing and impregnating them! So offensive, even outrageous, is such a concept that some Christian scholars have recast the whole event in purely human terms: 'sons of men' referring to godly humans and 'daughters of men', to the ungodly (Augustine and Chrysostom both dogmatically refused to take the story literally and claimed it to be a myth with a moral). Jewish expositors, however, are virtually unanimous in retaining the 'angelic' interpretation. It is ironic that Hollywood has recently produced a number of horror films which exploit the theme of demonic impregnation. The whole thing seems like a ghastly counterfeit of the virgin birth of Christ – though there are some fundamental differences (the Spirit who 'came on' Mary was holy rather than evil, Creator rather than creature and, above all, totally free of any sexual links with her).

Later Jewish tradition has embellished the biblical account with many additional details, particularly in the pseudepigraphal book of 'Enoch'. The culprits were called 'the Watchers' and were led by one named 'Azazel' (the same name as the Levitical scapegoat). The incident is located in the time of Jared, Enoch's father, and in the region of Mount Hermon. One result of the unnatural liaison was that the 'wives' learned the arts of occult magic. Another was the begetting of grotesque 'hybrid' offspring (Nephilim), who were physically superior (giants), but morally inferior (controlled by pride and lust, even given to cannibalism). Enoch, the first recorded prophet, predicted that God would come down with his faithful angels to deal with this bizarre situation (Jude 14f provides inspired endorsement for this aspect, at least). The archangel Gabriel slew the giants (they certainly disappeared), while another, Raphael, bound Azazel.

Such is the background to the references in these letters of Peter and Jude, who appear to accept the Genesis account in its entirety and much of the apocryphal expansion of it in 'Enoch'. There is a remarkable similarity between their separate treatments of the incident, suggesting some mutual correlation of a verbal or literary nature, or at least a shared indebtedness to a common source (as in the case of Isa 2:2–4 and Mic 4:1–3). Whatever the relation between them, the event is peripheral rather than central in both writings, only one example among a number of others (the rest are undoubtedly historical events). The following four aspects are highlighted.

First, the nature of their sin. Their unseemly act was a gross violation of God's established order of creation. The angels had abandoned their proper position and therefore their authority (which was delegated, not inherent). Such abuse of privilege is an 'abomination' to the Creator, comparable to human intercourse with animals (Lev 18:23; 20:15), though that carried no possibility of fertilisation. The beauty of creation is utterly distorted by such perversion. It is of the essence of sin to change our appointed station and rank, whether in a downward or upward direction (cf 'you will be like God' in Gen 3:5).

Second, the motive behind it. The root of the problem was uncontrolled sexual desire, beginning with the undisciplined use of the faculty of sight. This 'lust of the eyes' (1 John 2:16) so often leads to sin (Gen 3:6; Josh 7:21; Judg 14:1; 2 Sam 11:2). Job fought against it successfully (Job 31:1). Jesus gave one of his most solemn warnings about it (Matt 5:28f). Both Peter and Jude were concerned that false teachers were corrupting believers by preaching and practising such immorality, whose justification for it was that the grace of God would cover it, thus 'turning the grace of God into a licence for immorality' (Jude 4). At its worst, such teaching actually encouraged people to sin so that they could receive more grace (Paul faced the same problem; Rom 6:1). It is an all too familiar distortion of the gospel which makes justification essential, but sanctification optional. Significantly, the false teachers, like the rebel angels, despised authority.

Third, the certainty of judgement. God did not allow the situation to continue indefinitely (though his amazing patience did give time for their illegitimate offspring to be produced). Because God does not judge immediately, that should not lead to complacency or presumption. Because he is holy, he must ultimately eradicate evil. 'The mills of God grind slowly, yet they grind exceeding small' (Friedrich von Logau). The angels no more escaped their just deserts than did Sodom and Gomorrah (the next example of immorality in both Peter and Jude).

Fourth, the delay in their punishment. Though there are still other 'unclean spirits' in our world, these particular angels have been removed from it and are prevented from ever repeating their crime. They have been taken into custody and are being kept in the lowest, darkest dungeons, in chains. To describe this place, Peter borrows a word from Greek legend ('tartarus'), presumably because its meaning would be familiar to his readers from their background and would communicate the appropriate horror and revulsion. But both authors emphasise that this imprisonment is not their final punishment. They are simply awaiting trial, meanwhile restrained from creating further havoc. The devil is still at liberty, though he will also be confined in the same way and in the same place during the 'millennium' and before the final judgement (Rev 20:1-3, where 'the abyss' is probably the same as 'tartarus'; see Scripture Study J).

To conclude, it is important to underline the fact that neither author introduced this unsavoury topic to encourage intellectual curiosity but to ensure moral consistency. This was the very practical reason, indeed the only reason, why they referred to this bizarre series of events – and it should be our main reason for studying it. Both were concerned to combat a disastrous incursion of sexual immorality into Christian fellowships they had known and served.

The basic premise of their appeal is the immutable character of God. He has not changed throughout time or eternity. Whether his commands are disobeyed by angelic or human beings, whether before Noah or after Christ, whether among unbelievers or believers, God will always take sin seriously and ultimately punish it, if it has not been confessed, forgiven, renounced and abandoned. No one is exempt, for he has no favourites; his judgement is utterly impartial (Rom 2:1-11). Judgement begins with his own family (1 Pet 4:17). There is a wholesome fear of God (1 Pet 2:17) which will motivate believers to make their calling and election sure, in order to receive a rich welcome into the eternal kingdom of our Lord and Saviour Jesus Christ (2 Pet 1:10f; verses 3-9 tell us exactly how to do this). If we don't learn the lesson of the fallen angels, we shall end up by joining them.

SCRIPTURE STUDY J:
THE FINAL JUDGEMENT

Read Rev 20:1–15.

The Bible is a book of history, yet it is unlike any other. It starts earlier and finishes later, stretching from the beginning to the end of time. Since man can neither observe nor record the events of the distant past or future, the first and last chapters of scripture present a challenge to the enquiring mind. They are either human speculation or divine revelation.

It has become fashionable to treat early Genesis and late Revelation as 'myth', narratives with spiritual but without historical significance, edifying for the present, but not enlightening about the past or the future. They must be 'de-mythologised' for modern thought, stripped of their temporal framework to reveal their eternal verities. Fables contain truths, but not facts.

Behind this apparent sophistication lies the humanist reluctance to believe anything beyond the reach of our own faculties and reason. That God should know more than man is offensive; that God should show us what he knows is beyond credulity. Prophecy is as 'impossible' as miracle in our closed space-time continuum, especially when it 'foretells' events that have not happened yet with any detailed accuracy.

So the question of faith must be considered before studying prophetic scriptures. Do we believe God can know the future as we know the past? Even more important, do we believe he knows because he is in control of the future and has already decided what he is going to do with it?

This is not to commit intellectual suicide. Faith and reason can be travelling companions, but there comes a point down the road where faith must go ahead and lead reason, or the road becomes a cul-de-sac without reaching full and final reality.

The twentieth chapter of the book of Revelation is a classic case. Purporting to predict some of the last events in human history, albeit in unfamiliar terms, the reader is challenged to decide whether these are historical (happening once in the future) or existential (happening continuously all the time).

The central prediction is the judgement of the whole human race, including both those already dead and those still surviving at the time. Is this a 'picture' of the fact that we are being 'judged' every moment of our lives by our reactions and attitudes? Is it a reminder that each one of us will be separately 'judged' at the moment of death, when change and development cease? Or does it refer to a single event yet to come, when we will all be 'judged' together?

Christian orthodoxy has consistently held to the third interpretation: there is to be a 'Day of Judgement' at the very end of history. The eternal destiny of 'the quick [the living] and the dead' will be decided on that great occasion. Though the word 'day' is not used in this particular passage, it is widely used in both Old and New Testaments when referring to this climactic crisis (cf Joel 2:31; Acts 2:20; 2 Thess 2:2f; 2 Tim 1:12; 4:8).

Accepting this key prediction as fact rather than fable, truth rather than myth, it is therefore surprising that some Christians have such problems with the other predictions in this chapter. They treat the main event as literal, but consider the preceding and following events as 'metaphorical', or even mythical. Some consistency of faith is surely more appropriate. The whole programme of final happenings is presented in sequential order and unbroken style. There is no internal textual reason for taking one event as literal and another as metaphorical. The whole should be taken one way or the other. Any selectivity must be subjective, revealing the presuppositions and prejudices (in the sense of prejudgements) of the selector.

The chapter may be analysed according to the three dimensions of time: what happens before, during and after the final judgement. Most Christian controversy focuses on the first (the so-called 'millennium'); there is a large consensus on the second; but there is a growing doubt about the third (the 'lake of fire'), which is, of course, our primary topic. In the interests of wholeness, we shall examine all three in some detail.

BEFORE THE JUDGEMENT

The phrases 'And I saw . . . I saw . . . Then I saw . . .' (vv. 1,4,11) clearly indicate a sequence of visions intended to convey a sequence of events, as they do in the previous chapter (19:11,17,19). Remember that chapter divisions were never part of the original text; since the two chapters really belong together as a continuous narrative, we must glance at the earlier one to get into the flow of events.

In it the 'King of Kings and Lord of Lords', also called 'the Word of God' (and surely referring to Jesus Christ), comes from heaven (on a horse of war, not a donkey of peace) to deal with all his enemies on earth. The return of Jesus to planet earth is referred to over three hundred times in the New Testament (the cross is mentioned about the same number of times, making these two events the two 'poles' of New Testament thought). He then defeats an international coalition of kings and their armies, killing them all (with his word alone), thus consigning them to hades. The two evil world leaders (the political 'beast' and the religious 'false prophet') are immediately sent to hell (even before the 'Day of Judgement', so the 'lake of fire' must be fully 'prepared' at that stage). So all those who have plotted against the Lord's 'anointed' (Ps 2:2, the only verse in the Psalms to contain the Hebrew word: *meschiah*; note that v.9 is quoted in Rev 19:15) have been overthrown and removed from the earth – except one, the devil. What is to be done with him?

At this point, there is a development so unexpected that it has the 'ring of truth' about it (being so unlikely to have occurred to human reason or imagination). The devil, here given all four titles already used of him in this book (dragon, serpent, devil and Satan), is treated quite differently from all those he has used to defy and disrupt God's purposes on earth. He is not killed with the kings and armies (he cannot be, for he is a fallen 'angel' and 'cannot die'; Luke 20:36). Nor is he thrown into the 'lake of fire' with his two henchmen, the beast and the false prophet. Instead, he is taken into custody and consigned to 'the abyss' (or, 'the pit'), the deepest, darkest place in the present universe, dreaded by all the demons (Luke 8:31), where some of them have already been incarcerated since the time of Noah's flood (2 Pet 2:4, here the place is called 'tartarus'; see Scripture Study I). Dreadful though it is to be chained in such a prison, this is not considered as the devil's punishment; he is merely being kept under restraint. In passing, we note that he is apprehended by another angel, not the Lord (the final indignity?) and that the arrest takes place on earth (the angel had to come 'down out of heaven').

Even more astonishing, this confinement is temporary rather than permanent. It is only for 'a thousand years' (whether taken as an exact number or a round figure, it is clearly a considerable period of time). Then he will be given his freedom again (though for a brief space of time), returning to his old ways of deceiving human beings into thinking they can and should get rid of God's people on earth. Who would have imagined such a train of events?

There is much more to be said about this 'millennium' (the Latin word for a thousand years, the Greek equivalent being *chilios*; from these come the theological labels 'millennianism' and 'chiliasm'). On the negative side, all the powerful enemies of Christ, both human and demonic, will have been removed from the earth, no longer able to influence human affairs. That alone would bring about a radical change in the course of history. But it would leave a power vacuum. Who would take over the responsibility of government?

On the positive side, the world will be ruled by God's anointed king, the 'Christ' (the word is used on its own here and is the title of the expected Jewish Messiah) and the 'ministers' to whom he has given authority to administer justice. Those who have 'endured' for him in earlier times will now 'reign' with him (2 Tim 2:12); the 'saints will judge the world' (1 Cor 6:2). God's people, suppressed by governments of the world for so long, will then be the world government! Single-handed, Christ will have achieved the greatest revolution of all, enabling the meek to inherit the earth, as he and his mother had prophesied (Matt 5:5; Luke 1:52).

Among the new rulers of the earth, John 'the seer' particularly notices one special group ('And I saw . . .' in v.4b marks a new vision and distinguishes it from v.4a). Those who had been martyred in the last terrible dictatorship and who refused to compromise their faith, even to obtain the necessities of life (Rev 13:16f), have now taken the place of their persecutor. What a reward for their costly fidelity!

It is obvious from this last group that a resurrection must have taken place before this 'millennium', and not with old bodies but with new ones (that would live a thousand years and more). This is now specifically stated: there are, in fact, to be two resurrections, the 'first' of those qualified to reign with Christ and then, much later, 'the rest of the dead'. Those who are raised in the 'first' are blessed and holy, blessed because they have been holy. They will then also know for certain that there is no possibility that they could later be sentenced to the 'second death' on the Day of Judgement; the very fact of their early resurrection and reign with Christ has settled the issue of their eternal destiny beyond all possible doubt (is this what Paul was referring to when he talked about 'attaining to the resurrection *out from* among the dead' by knowing the fellowship of Christ's sufferings and the power of his resurrection? Phil 3:10f). Those who are so 'blessed' will become priests as well as kings, mediators as well as monarchs, on the earth (Rev 5:10).

One can only imagine what peace and prosperity will result from such a world government. With Christ and his perfected people in control, acknowledged by the entire population, the kingdoms of the world will have become the kingdom of our Lord and of his Christ (Rev 11:15). Righteousness will flow through society like a river. That persistent hope of the human race, the 'Golden Age', will have arrived. Truly, paradise will have been regained. Such an idyllic existence would surely be heaven on earth and could go on for ever.

But appearances can be deceptive. An ideal government and environment may satisfy the human desire for peace and prosperity, but they do not change human nature. People may be happy with a benevolent dictatorship when it brings such obvious benefits – until they are offered the chance of freedom from that authority. Incredibly, when at the end of the millennium the devil is again free to influence human affairs, he is still able to plant hatred for the people and places associated with God. He gathers forces from the four corners of the earth to make a final bid for independence from the Creator of the universe. This time God himself, not Christ, destroys the vast human army (and with fire rather than word). The indestructible devil is finally given his deserts and thrown into the 'lake of fire', joining his two henchmen already there (for what then happens to him, see below).

Such is the extraordinary series of events *before* the Day of Judgement, if this passage is taken at face value. It is not easy to imagine such things happening and even more difficult to understand why they should. We are not told, and any attempt to explain it runs the risk of speculation. Yet two results of the 'millennium' may also indicate the reasons.

On the one hand, the reign of Christ and its benefits will be tangibly and visibly demonstrated in the very sphere where they were rejected. This would be entirely consistent with the God who vindicates the righteous. This world has seen only too clearly the results of Satan's reign; surely it ought to see what it can be like in the hands of the Son of God. After all, our world was always intended to be a gift of the Father to his Son and it is God's purpose to 'bring all things in heaven *and on earth* together under one head, even Christ' (Eph 1:10). It is entirely congruous that the Father should want to manifest this on the old earth, before it passes away and gives place to the new.

On the other hand, the 'millennium' will also clearly demonstrate that a change of government is not the final solution to the world's problems. A perfect sovereign needs perfect subjects if there is to be a perfect kingdom. Outward acquiescence is not the same as inward acceptance. The final tragedy in the 'millennium' reveals that human nature, even under ideal conditions, is still vulnerable to offers of autonomy, as it was in the garden of Eden.

This dual demonstration, of Christ's power for good and Satan's power for evil, is a fitting prelude to the Day of Judgement. The issue is clarified, the alternatives fully exposed. As there are only two rulers in this world, there will be only two destinies in the next. Ultimately, we spend eternity with Christ or with Satan. It is black and white; there are no shades of grey.

However, before looking at the day when this division will be made, we must pause to consider the fact that Christians are often deeply divided over the 'millennium' that precedes it, many feeling quite unable to accept the scenario we have just described. They point out that this is the only New Testament passage that clearly mentions it, and even then in a book which is said to be 'obscure', full of apocalyptic imagery and unfamiliar symbols. It is therefore considered inappropriate to take the book as a whole, or even parts of it, as a literal description of future events. It must not, then, be used as a source of data for eschatological doctrine.

In response, we may point out that this chapter, while it has a few puzzling details ('Gog and Magog', for example, the name given to the last coalition army to attack Jerusalem; it could simply be too early for us to identify these), is nevertheless for the most part in clear, straightforward language. It is not difficult to understand, even if some find it hard to accept. Furthermore, even if this is the *only* clear reference to a millennium, it is at least a *clear* reference. Is that not enough? How often does God have to say something before we believe it? It is hardly surprising that it is 'only' mentioned here, since Revelation is the only book in the New Testament dealing with the end of time in any detail (as Genesis is the only Old Testament book dealing with the beginning of time). Revelation is also our only source of any detailed information about the new heaven and earth and the new Jerusalem. Why do those who are sceptical about the millennium usually accept chapters 21 and 22 without question? Probably because it's easier to believe amazing things in another world than in this one!

The more positive answer to such scepticism is to ask how the inspired writer and his readers would understand this revelation. We begin by pointing out that he and many of them were Jews. The whole book is thoroughly Jewish, steeped in Hebrew 'apocalyptic' (that branch of prophecy which 'unveiled' the future in pictorial style) and packed with direct and indirect references to the Jewish scriptures. It has been said that a knowledge of the Old Testament is absolutely essential to understanding Revelation (which may explain why so many Christians find it perplexing!).

But there is more to the Jewish background than their canonical scriptures, the last of which (Malachi) was written four hundred years before Revelation was penned. Their thinking about the future made enormous strides during those 'inter-Testament' centuries, possibly as a result of their Babylonian exile and the challenge of contact with other religions (notably Zoroastrianism) which had a highly developed programme of the 'end-times', including belief in resurrection, judgement, heaven and hell. The Jewish people must have been challenged to think through their own 'eschatology' (i.e. theology of the future, from the Greek word: *eschaton*, which means 'the end').

Among the Jews, the Pharisees had the clearest 'scheme', while the Sadducees were more sceptical. But Jewish eschatology generally had advanced far beyond the hints in their scriptures and may be found in the 'apocryphal' (the word means 'hidden' and refers to those books kept out of the 'canon' or 'rule' of scripture) and 'pseudepigraphal' (anonymous writings over the assumed name of a well-known Old Testament figure, such as Moses) writings between the two Testaments. In particular, the books of Baruch and Esdras reveal their expectations about the 'last days'.

From these, emerges a remarkably similar picture to that described in Revelation. At least some Jews, if not many, already believed that before the advent of a new heaven and earth (promised in Isa 65:17), there would be a Messianic 'age' on earth, when the Lord's 'anointed' (Hebrew: *meschiah*; Greek: *christos*) would rule the nations. Speculation about the duration of this Messianic rule on earth varied, but at least one source mentions a thousand years. They had even worked out that this would involve *two* resurrections, the first taking place at the beginning of the 'age' and referred to as the 'resurrection of the righteous' (Jesus himself used this phrase when talking to Pharisees; Luke 14:14).

There is little basic difference between this hope and the 'millennium' in Revelation. Though its detailed description is found outside the inspired words of the Old Testament, it is endorsed in the inspired words of the New Testament. John was not communicating an entirely original concept; Jewish readers would easily recognise it. But he was expanding their understanding of it: in particular, by identifying Jesus as the coming ruler and including the banishment of Satan, neither of which was part of the Jewish expectation.

It would be no surprise, therefore, to find that the Jewish segment of the early church understood the 'millennium' quite literally, since that hope was already part of their heritage. Such, indeed, was the case. What is also clear is that the Gentile segment adopted the same understanding. Most references to the subject by Christian writers in the first few centuries (collectively known as 'the Fathers') were 'millennialists' (interested readers may begin with Justin Martyr or Irenaeus, in the second century). They believed in 'the corporeal reign of Christ on this very earth' (to quote Papias, bishop of Hierapolis in Asia), often associating it with the restoration of a kingdom to Israel (thus Justin Martyr, though not all agreed with him).

This early consensus is now referred to as the *pre-millennial* position (because it holds that Christ will return *before* setting up his kingdom on earth). This hope began to fade in the third and fourth centuries, perhaps because it was becoming clear that the Lord's return was not going to be as soon as had been expected. By the fifth century, Augustine, bishop of Hippo in northern Africa, was teaching a revised (reversed?) programme, in which Jesus would return *after* his kingdom has been established on earth (so this is known as the *post-millennial* position). Undoubtedly, this more optimistic scenario was fostered by the changed fortunes of the church. Roman persecution had ended; the Emperor himself (Constantine) had been converted and the Christian faith had become the official 'established' religion. As the Empire declined and fell, the church appeared to be taking its place as a world power (the bishop of Rome adopted the former Emperor's title 'Pontifex Maximus', as well as other trappings). The church was taking the form of a kingdom, which would later be known as 'Christendom'. The new Jerusalem was being built on earth, by the church (Augustine's most influential book was entitled: *The City of God*). The vision of an international church-state, that would last a thousand years until the King returned, captured the ecclesiastical imagination. Thomas Aquinas picked up this torch and it has remained the official teaching of the Roman Catholic church (one reason why the Vatican is a political state), though there is understandably some debate about when this millennial reign began or will begin.

The Protestant reformers did not emphasise eschatology, so their views are not clear. They seem to have adopted and adapted the 'post-millennial' outlook of their time, transferring it to the Protestant state-churches and identifying the Pope and his church-state as the scarlet whore of Babylon, the very opposite of the city of God.

How do post-millennialists handle Revelation 20? They do see it as a literal period of time on earth, though they do not seem quite clear whether it has begun yet. The emphasis is on the body of the church, rather than its Head, as the agent who binds the devil and establishes the kingdom. The 'first' resurrection is usually seen as that of Christ himself. The total absence of the beast, the false prophet, and even the devil himself is usually avoided or explained as referring to the church, rather than the world. For obvious reasons, this view does not put any emphasis on the imminence of Christ's return.

To return to our brief historical survey, as the 'Enlightenment' (or 'Renaissance') spread its humanist and secularist influence over Europe, it became increasingly difficult for Christians to believe that the millennium had already begun (or even would ever come before Christ returned). The reality was that the church, Catholic or Protestant, was no longer the dominating influence in the Western world, to say nothing of 'heathen' lands elsewhere. To claim that the devil was no longer deceiving anyone flew in the face of the facts.

Instead of returning to the 'classic' pre-millennial position of the early church, which had long since been largely forgotten, a third view appeared, which effectively removed the millennium not only from the end of history but from earthly history (hence it is known as the *a-millennial* position, the prefix virtually meaning 'non-'). The 'reign' of Christ has already begun in *heaven* and covers the whole period between his ascension and return (and has already lasted two millennia, so the 'thousand' of scripture is a symbolic number). The binding of Satan took place during Christ's first visit to earth. The 'first' resurrection takes place whenever a person is born again and 'raised from death to life'. Only the 'second' is a bodily resurrection, which will happen when Christ returns to take his people to heaven, the eternal kingdom. The absence of beast, false prophet and devil refers to heaven and not earth. With no Messianic rule on earth, Christ's second visit will be extremely brief (indeed, one cannot help asking why he should come back at all; why not give believers their new bodies in heaven?).

The 'a-millennialist' tends to see the pre-/post- debate as an irrelevant distraction ('a plague on both your houses'), tending to despise both or at least regard his own position as the most enlightened.

159

The last one hundred and fifty years have seen an increased expectancy of the Lord's return (not least because of the accelerating increase of cataclysmic events on a global scale) and, with it, a revival of pre-millennianism – but in a new framework, known as 'dispensationalism', which combines the 'classic' view of the early church with some novel, even eccentric features. Stemming from the teaching of J.N. Darby (founder of the Plymouth Brethren), disseminated through Notes in the Scofield Bible and now popularised through Hal Lindsay's books, this scheme divides history into distinct periods (called 'dispensations'), each of which has its own characteristic basis for the relationship between God and man. The 'millennium' is seen as the last dispensation of history and is understood to be the 'kingdom' which Jesus tried, but failed, to bring to Israel on his first visit. The reign inaugurated by his second visit will be as 'King of the Jews', all Christians having been 'raptured' to heaven some years before the end of the previous dispensation (and before the 'Great Tribulation' during which the antichrist will reign on earth – hence the term 'pre-Tribulation rapture'). The heart of 'dispensationalism' is its radical division between Christian and Jewish destinies, the 'kingdom' belonging to the latter on earth, while the former are in heaven. Even this extremely brief summary should be enough to show how different this is from the early church's thinking.

It is a great pity that most contemporary Christians have only heard the 'pre-millennial' case in this grossly distorted form and have thrown out the 'classic' baby with the 'dispensational' bath-water! Those brought up on dispensational teaching have often swung from a 'kingdom' that is entirely future and Jewish to one that is entirely present and has no place for Israel. Such seems to have happened with 'Restoration' and 'Dominion' theologies, both of which appear to be moving towards a post-millennial optimism with its corresponding decline of emphasis on the Second Coming as the focus of Christian hope. Fortunately, some eminent scholars are recovering and communicating the 'classic' pre-millennial outlook, free from its dispensational distortion; they deserve a hearing (the writings of George Eldon Ladd, Merrill Tenney and J. Barton Payne are particularly helpful).

Many have grown tired of the whole discussion, partly because extreme polarisation has made it an issue of fellowship, endangering the unity of true believers, and partly because its relevance is not readily obvious (a friend of mine called the whole debate 'a pre-post-erous preoccupation'!). A new label has been coined, *pan-millennial*, to cover those who simply believe that 'everything will pan out alright in the end'! Originally intended as a joke, there is some truth in the label, which is very appropriate for those who are simply not bothered to engage in any serious study of the subject. In other words, they simply ignore it, convinced there are many better things to be doing. But ignoring it does not remove it from the Word of God; and if *all* scripture is inspired and useful (2 Tim 3:16), it is there for a purpose. It is therefore valid to ask why it is there and what is its meaning. To totally ignore it is equivalent to erasing it and comes perilously near deserving the curse on 'anyone who takes words away from this book of prophecy' (Rev 22:19).

Having said all this, one's view of the 'millennium' hardly affects one's thinking about hell, which is the main topic before us. Indeed, its only bearing on the subject is the entry date of its first inhabitants. Three are thrown into the 'lake of fire' *before* the Day of Judgement, two of them (the 'beast' and the 'false prophet') before the 'millennium'. Those who locate the millennium in the present era of church history (as both the post-millennialist and a-millennialist do) must explain this unusual fact – as well as the greater problem presented by the clear statement that for most of the period, Satan, though not yet in hell, is totally isolated from the earth. Incidentally, there is no mention of exactly when the devil's angels join him in hell, though it looks as if that too will be before any human beings are sent there (Matt 25:41).

DURING THE JUDGEMENT

Little need be said here, since Christians are largely agreed that this is a literal event taking place at the end of time.

The earthly environment rapidly disappears, leaving only its inhabitants before their Maker (the very opposite view to many pessimistic ecologists, who believe the inhabitants will disappear first, leaving only a polluted environment).

All the dead will be raised, no matter what happened to their earthly bodies (whether properly interred in the ground or drowned in the sea; the complete disintegration of physical remains in no way prevents resurrection, a fact relevant to questions about cremation). Social rank will be irrelevant, 'great and small' standing side by side.

The throne of judgement is white (the colour of purity) and the Judge is both divine and human (the unidentified 'him' could be understood as God, but scripture clearly indicates that he has delegated this responsibility to his Son; Matt 25:31f; John 5:27; Acts 17:31; Rom 2:16; 2 Cor 5:10; Rev 5:6).

Whether the 'books' are literal or symbolic, their message is clear. A record has been kept of everything done (and said) by everyone who has ever lived. Unlike the popular television show *This is Your Life*, there will be no sympathetic selection for public presentation, no omission of things best kept hidden. All will be revealed. No excuses or appeals will be uttered in the light of such damning evidence.

If these were the only books opened, who could possibly be acquitted? The entire human race must surely be condemned (Rom 3:9–18). But there is one other book to be opened. It belongs to the Judge himself; his own name is on it and his own deeds are recorded in it. His is the one life lived on earth without a single indictable offence (which qualifies him to be the Judge of all other human beings; John 8:7). All other books spell death for their subjects; his alone is the book of life, for he alone deserves to live.

Yet there are many other names in this book, under his own. They are the names of those who put their faith in him and have kept faith with him (by remaining faithful to him). For his name's sake they have 'overcome' the world, the flesh and the devil, so their names have remained in the book and not been erased (Rev 3:5). They have not disowned him, so he will not now disown them (Matt 10:33; 2 Tim 2:12).

The impression is left of a simple act of judgement, quite unlike earthly court scenes with their endless weighing of testimony and evidence. Justice will be done and be seen to be done. The books need only be opened. The guilty are condemned by their own autobiographies. The acquitted are covered by the Judge's biography. It is an awesome scene of eternal significance.

The results are also simple. The human race is divided into two groups: the old humanity in Adam and the new humanity in Christ, 'Home sapiens' and 'Homo novus'. Only two destinies lie ahead, only two places have been prepared for the future existence of their resurrected bodies.

AFTER THE JUDGEMENT

The two destinies have already been fully discussed (in chapters 3 and 6). The new heaven and earth are described in the last two chapters of Revelation. Here, in chapter 20, we have some of the clearest statements in scripture about hell itself. Three aspects are important.

First, 'death' and 'hades' are themselves thrown into the 'lake of fire'. The event which causes our spirits to become disembodied and the place which holds disembodied spirits are both abolished; the one will never happen again, so that the other will never again be needed. Henceforth, all human spirits will have a bodily existence; this will be their permanent state. Many have not noticed that Jesus talked about hell (or Gehenna) as a place for people with bodies (Matt 5:29f; 10:28). Since 'death' and 'hades' are things rather than persons, having no consciousness of themselves, it is assumed that being thrown into the fire signifies their total extinction. But does the fire do the same to persons?

Second, the 'lake of fire' is called 'the second death'. At first sight, this phrase might be thought to imply the extinction of persons. As the 'first' death brought the body to the end of its existence (more or less), does the 'second' bring body and soul to the end of their existence? But this is not the whole story about the first death. It may have brought the body to dissolution, but it certainly did not end the existence of the self-conscious person who had inhabited it. Why should the 'second death' do so? Furthermore, the first death was a judicial rather than a natural occurrence, a punishment for sin (Gen 2:17). So is the 'second'. And the essence of both is *separation*. The first death separates us from other human beings, the second from the Divine Being. The heart of hell is that God is not there.

Third, hell is described as being 'tormented day and night for ever and ever'. This is the most unequivocal example of this terrible truth in the whole of the New Testament. Annihilationists have simply dismissed it as 'difficult' (only because it doesn't fit in with their opinion) or 'symbolic' (without a word about what they think it symbolises). Could there be a plainer statement? 'Tormented' can only mean conscious suffering; 'day and night' can only mean without respite; and 'for ever and ever' (literally, 'to the ages of the ages', the strongest Greek expression to convey 'everlastingness') can only mean inconceivably endless.

However, it has been pointed out that this statement is applied to the devil rather than human beings. But it also includes his two human henchmen, who, it says, have already experienced this 'torment' for the thousand years of the millennium. However, some refuse to accept that these are human or even personal, claiming them to be 'personifications' of impersonal social structures and institutions which 'oppress' human society. How such can be 'tormented' is not explained. Nor is the fact that in the Bible there are many other 'antichrists' and 'false prophets' in scripture (1 John 2:18; Matt 24:11), every one of whom is clearly a personal human being. However, earlier in this book it is said of those who accept the 'trade-mark' of the 'beast' in order to buy and sell (and surely these are human beings): 'And the smoke of their torment rises for ever and ever. There is no rest day or night' (Rev 14:11). The language is identical for both human and demonic beings alike – conscious torment with neither temporary respite nor permanent release.

What clinches it is Jesus' own teaching in the 'parable' of the sheep and goats (Matt 25:31-46; see Scripture Study A). The goats on the King's left hand (no one ever doubts that these are human beings) are not only sent to the same *place* as the devil and his angels, but into the same *punishment*, which is 'eternal'. There is not even a hint that the fire which 'torments' the fallen angels, for whom it was originally prepared, will prove to be a 'merciful release' to those who join them. As will all those whose names are not found written in the book of life (Rev 20:15). On which sober note we conclude our study.